CHARIOTS OF THE GOSPEL

CHARIOTS
OF THE
GOSPEL

The Centenary History of the Church Army

DONALD LYNCH

H. E. WALTER LTD

First published in 1982 by
H. E. Walter Ltd
26 Grafton Road, Worthing
West Sussex BN11 1QU, England

ISBN 0 85479 044 6

*Printed in Great Britain by
Eyre & Spottiswoode Limited
at Grosvenor Press, Portsmouth*

CONTENTS

LIST OF ILLUSTRATIONS

FOREWORD

The Church's task has always been two-fold: to worship and to evangelise. That will continue to be its task so long as it is the Church militant. Sometimes its vision grows dim. At such times God finds ways of raising up men and institutions to re-kindle its passion to serve him.

A century ago he did just this through Wilson Carlile and the Church Army which he founded and served. For a hundred years and through a complete social revolution and two world wars, the Church Army has held to its course, adapting itself to changing conditions and needs but seeking to keep true to its primary calling.

Its purpose is to proclaim the Good News by word and action, to bring wholeness to those who are damaged by sin and want, to train and deploy evangelists within the Church's ministry, and to help Christians to express their faith intelligently and winsomely.

The story of this work needed to be told concisely. Who better to do it than Donald Lynch, who from the beginning of his ministry had close links with the Church Army and from 1953—60 was Principal of its Training College and from 1960—75 its Chief Secretary?

I greatly welcome this book and hope it will be widely read. Long may the Church Army continue to do its part in keeping the Church true to the commission given to it by its Master.

Donald Coggan
Lately Archbishop of Canterbury

PREFACE

He scored a century . . . She lived to be a hundred . . .
A hundred miles an hour . . . A century of service . . .
There is a completeness about the number 100. It seems to
be a natural landmark in history and so we talk about the
eighteenth or nineteenth century as a convenient measurement
of time. Dictionaries define a hundred as ten decades. This
book written for the centenary of the Church Army covers
the history of that Society roughly in ten year periods. It
does not work out exactly. In particular the two decades
between the wars do not lend themselves to separate descriptions. I feel inclined to write E. & O. E. at the end of the book
because there are many omissions and probably not a few
errors. My thanks are due to many members of Church Army
staff who have answered my queries and supplied information
and in particular to Sister Joan Wilbourne, the Church Army
Archivist. My thanks are still more due to my wife who has
deciphered my manuscript and typed it for the publisher.

The title of the book was suggested by third century descriptions of Christ as a charioteer driving his chariot, the Church.
This image appears in the writings of Clement of Alexandria
and Origen and can be seen on a mosaic in Rome which was
made soon after the year 300. I am indebted to Canon Professor Henry Chadwick for this information.

St. George's Day, 1982   Donald Lynch

CHAPTER ONE

THE FOUNDER

His family and friends

'War declared on Sin and Satan under the command of the Rev. W. Carlile, every night at 8 o'clock. Come if you dare'. So ran a handbill used by the Church Army in 1883, a few months after its foundation. We may use different language today, but *'War on Sin and Satan'* sums up what the Church Army has always stood for.

The early history of the Church Army is the life story of this one man, Wilson Carlile, who personally led the Church Army for sixty of its hundred years. Though he was not physically strong as a child he was a born fighter. Whenever he saw people defeated by sin and adversity his heart went out to them and he went into action. As well as being a fighter he was also a leader. It has been said that leadership is the art of inducing other people to believe that they want to go in the same direction as you are going. The evidence for this, so far as Wilson Carlile is concerned, is to be seen in the lives of many people who through his preaching and example committed themselves to Christ and to the battle against evil.

Wilson Carlile was born at Brixton on the 14th of January, 1847, into a family which can trace its history to the days before the Norman Conquest. The name is derived from the City of Carlisle where Hildred, the brother of King Duncan I of Scotland, was Baron. He became known by the local name, which was spelt in various ways, the most picturesque being Sir Hildred de Karliolo. The family also had distant connections by marriage with the royal houses of England and France.

For several centuries the Carliles lived in the Lowlands of

Scotland, some of them in Torthorwald Castle, part of which still stands in ruin. The branch of the family to which Wilson Carlile belonged was associated with Annan, and moved to Paisley in the middle of the 18th century. Several Carliles held office as Baillie or Provost in Annan and Paisley. The family business at Paisley was the manufacture of linen and cotton thread.

Early in the 19th century Wilson Carlile's grandfather moved to London and established a warehouse business (Carlile Pittman & Co) in Bow Lane, Cheapside, of which Wilson's father (Edward Carlile 1819—1901) became head. In 1845 Edward married Maria Louisa Wilson (1825—1908) the daughter of another merchant in the City of London who was head of Benjamin Wilson & Co. Her family had Scottish origins in Midlothian and Fife.

For generations most of the Carlile family had been devout Christians. Coming from Scottish Presbyterian stock they took a while to move from English non-conformity to Anglicanism, and for some years Wilson Carlile and his parents were members of Stockwell Congregational Church. Wilson's uncle (James William Carlile) was a prosperous business man who took a keen interest in such church societies as The Bible Society, the Church Missionary Society, the Church Army and the Colonial and Continental Church Society, and in Ridley Hall and Wycliffe Hall. He served as Deputy Lieutenant and High Sheriff of Hertfordshire 1882—3. Edward Carlile became Churchwarden of St. Mary Aldermary in the City of London and also of Holy Trinity, Richmond. He was a keen supporter of the Church Army, Master of a City Livery Company (Haberdashers) and an active participant in local government in Richmond. His wife was a gifted linguist and was familiar with New Testament Greek as well as speaking fluent French and having a working knowledge of other European languages.

Wilson Carlile was the eldest of 12 children (three of whom died in childhood). His brother Sir Edward Hildred Carlile (1852—1942) was a director of J. & P. Coats Ltd in Huddersfield the firm which had absorbed the Carlile family business in 1887. He built a new wing for the Huddersfield Infirmary to commemorate the Diamond Jubilee of Queen Victoria. He was Member of Parliament for the St. Albans Division of

Hertfordshire and held the seat until 1919. Hildred was Chairman of the Board of Trade Committee on Work of National Importance from 1916–1919. In 1919 he was made a C.B.E. and was High Sheriff of Hertfordshire in 1922. Wilson and Hildred died on the same day in 1942.

Hildred and his sisters were deeply involved in Christian missionary and welfare work, and in particular Marie Louise gave her whole life to the service of the Church Army.

Wilson married Flora Vickers in 1870. She was a patient, self-effacing person, fond of music and singing, sharing her husband's faith, and content to give him her constant support. In the early days of their marriage they taught together classes of rough boys at Blackfriars and Richmond. Later on her time was fully occupied in the care of their five sons, born between 1872 and 1884. Four of the five took Cambridge degrees. Reginald, the youngest, died at Calgary in 1971. Victor and Edward took an active part in the work of the Church Army. Victor was officially Assistant Secretary for a period. In 1905 he accompanied his father on a visit to labour colonies in Denmark, Belgium, Holland and Germany to study continental methods of caring for vagrants, and on their return published jointly a book called *The Continental Outcast* (Published by T. Fisher Unwin 1906). In 1906 he visited Canada in connection with the Church Army scheme for emigrants. Edward was Honorary Appeals Secretary from 1927 to 1942 and a member of the Board from 1925 to 1940.

It is clear that Wilson Carlile had behind him on his father's side a long and distinguished family history, marked by involvement in business life and community service, and a strong Christian tradition. On his mother's side the family history is less well documented, but it is plain that it was from her that he received his interest and initial training in European languages (he could preach in French, German and Italian), and the encouragement of the musical ability which he showed at an early age and which he turned to such good use in Christian work.

As a child Wilson Carlile suffered from a spinal illness and was frequently laid up. He was educated at home until the age of eight and then attended a day school in Brixton. After a short period at the City of London School in 1860 he spent a year at a French School in Lille and then joined his maternal grandfather's firm Benjamin Wilson & Co.

CONVERSION

He set himself the target of making himself a fortune of £20,000 by the age of 25. He worked early and late. He was frugal and thrifty in his habits. He usually ran or cycled or rode on horseback to his office in the City. This served the double purpose of saving expense and giving him regular exercise, to alleviate his spinal weakness. Such spare time as he had he devoted to music. He developed great ability in the commercial world through attention to organisation and detail. At the age of eighteen he was virtually in charge of the firm and at the age of twenty-one the business was his. Even after his marriage and during the Franco-Prussian War (1870–71) he frequently travelled on the Continent in search of bargains. By 1873 he had achieved his objective and amassed his coveted £20,000 but shortly afterwards owing to a trade depression in which many City men were ruined, most of his fortune disappeared overnight. The shock of this revived some of his old physical weakness and sent him to his bed. This proved to be a blessing in disguise because it gave him time to think deeply about the purpose and direction of his life. Although his own religion did not go very deep he could not help being impressed by the faith of his parents. In his travels he had seen many young French and German soldiers going to almost certain death in battle and inevitably wondered whether death was the end. Then came the emotional disturbance of the failure of his business. One of his aunts sensed that the time was ripe, and left him a book called 'Grace and Truth' and said 'If ever you are worried about your soul read that.' Wilson Carlile found his aunt's visits irritating but one day he started to read the book. It changed his life. He described the experience thus: 'At the beginning of the chapter I was a rank outsider. Before I got to the end I had thrown myself at the feet of Christ and cried "My Lord and my God".'

He returned to business life for five years, as a partner in his father's firm, but his heart was no longer in money-making. He found his satisfaction in doing mission work amongst rough boys first of all in Plymouth Brethren circles at Blackfriars and then at Holy Trinity, Richmond. He and his wife were confirmed at Clapham Parish Church by Bishop Thorold of Rochester.

In 1875 he was involved in campaigns which D. L. Moody the American evangelist and Ira Sankey the musical director were conducting in Islington and Camberwell. He frequently accompanied the singing on the harmonium. He also trained the choir for the Camberwell campaign, and subsequently managed the London Evangelistic Choir which grew out of the Camberwell meetings. Through these experiences he learned some of the skills of evangelism and in particular of the part which music could play in winning people for Christ. One of Moody's associate evangelists was Professor Henry Drummond of Edinburgh from whom he learned a principle which he subsequently put into effect in the Church Army. Drummond rarely preached; instead he encouraged young men to speak briefly of their experiences of Christ. Carlile discovered that laymen could participate in this way in the proclamation of the Gospel.

In 1877 he felt sure of his vocation to be an evangelist and offered his services to the Evangelisation Society (founded in 1864). Here he gained some training and experience in preaching. Several volumes of his sermon notes of this period have survived, but it would be very difficult to reconstruct his addresses because they consist to a large extent of anecdotes which he obviously knew by heart and which appear in the notes in one or two words. One lucid example was an address given at a Brass Foundry at Kingston in December 1879. The brief notes indicate that he related his talk specifically to the interests of his audience.

1 Brass as a mirror (Exodus 38:8)
2 The Brazen Serpent (St. John 3:14)
3 Goliath's Armour and the Shield of Faith (I Samuel 17:5)
4 Christ's Pierced Feet (Revelation 2:18)

On paper it seems flat. But no doubt as he spoke the mirror flashed, the serpent came to life, David's battle was fought over again, and the crucified and glorified Christ uplifted vividly.

ORDINATION

In 1878 he was accepted by Dr. Thomas Boultbee as a student at St. John's College, Highbury. In those days it was unusual for a married man to enter a theological college. He lived at home in Richmond and travelled daily by train to Highbury reading constantly on the way. In spite of the grind of study when his real interest lay in preaching and in meeting human need, he completed the course in less than two years and was ordained by Bishop Jackson to the curacy at St. Mary Abbots, Kensington, with special responsibility for the daughter church of St. Paul.

It was a busy parish often with 50 baptisms and 30 weddings in a month and as many as 400 confirmations in a year. Kensington attracted him because as a result of his glimpse of military life in the Franco-Prussian war he was interested in soldiers and there was a barracks in the parish. He acted as Chaplain to the local workhouse where he was instrumental in the rehabilitation of residents who were capable of living independently. He conducted a weekly service for policemen, a force with which he always had happy relations.

St. Mary's proved to be an ideal place for him to commence his ministry because as a member of a large team consisting of the Vicar and ten curates representing all parties with the Church, he learned something of the comprehensiveness of the Church of England and tolerance of varying opinions.

He felt special concern for the poorer people who thronged the streets of Kensington but rarely worshipped in church. And so he entered the field of visual aids and started magic-lantern services in the school hall, and evening open-air meetings in Kensington High Street. These unorthodox methods drew considerable crowds. People came for various reasons; some to listen; some to pick pockets; some to start a fight and break up the meeting. But many of those who came for the fun of it found themselves faced with the call of Christ.

The open-air meetings were held after 9 at night when many people were strolling in the High Street, including coachmen, grooms, and servants in the large Kensington houses. At first Carlile had to do all the speaking, but it soon became impossible for him to do this on his own night after night, even with the support of friends who helped with the singing. He

Prebendary Wilson Carlile, C.H., D.D.

Miss Marie Louise Carlile

Above — Flying Column, late 19th century

Left — Dismissal of Crusaders outside Headquarters in Bryanston Street before the Great War

Below — Mission Caravan, 1911

gradually persuaded a few working men to take part in the meetings by reading out a verse of a hymn or a few sentences from the Bible, or by saying very simply the change that Jesus had made in their lives. In this way he built up a little group of men who talked about religion in the language of working men and by their sheer integrity won a hearing. After a time some of them would go off on their own and preach at street corners in the slums of North Kensington.

Sunday evenings were rather special. After Evensong, Carlile would lead a small procession through the streets to the Vestry Hall. The procession was often attacked by the Skeleton Army, a gang of roughs who enjoyed breaking up religious meetings. The Hall was usually full for a rowdy meeting with noisy hymns interspersed with brief talks by working people. At the end of the meeting Carlile invited any who wished to serve Christ to come and meet with him in the middle of the hall and for many men and women this was the beginning of a new life in Christ.

After some months the Vicar of St. Mary Abbots decided, in June 1882, that the open-air meetings must stop, because of the disruption of traffic and complaints lodged by local residents and shopkeepers. He encouraged his curate to continue similar work elsewhere, and the result was the foundation of the Church Army.

Carlile was naturally disappointed at having to terminate his work in Kensington but he described his conclusion as follows:

'Finding that both at the open-air and at the indoor meetings the timid exhortation and humble testimonies of working people attracted quite as much as did my own preaching, and that in fact they seemed to produce even a deeper effect on their own class, I felt I ought to go forth and try to train working men as Church evangelists and to band them together as duly authorised workers, some soldiers and some officers to assist in Church evangelisation.'

Wilson Carlile radiated his faith wherever he went, and did so with the utmost naturalness. He was humble and unselfconscious. He loved his Lord and he loved men. He was particularly fond of children. He had the ability to be equally at home with royalty or with prisoners. Another of his gifts was a lively imagination which enabled him to stand in other men's shoes and enter into their feelings and also to catch other men's imagination by the originality of his methods.

It was his opinion that a business training is one of the best beginnings for a clerical life. One of his great assets was his faith in the ability of ordinary people to bear active witness for Christ. He was always a man of action as well as of prayer. However unorthodox his methods of evangelism appeared to be he was deeply loyal to the Church of England and valued intensely its sacramental life.

COLLEAGUES

Wilson Carlile's great vision was to use working men as evangelists to their fellows, but to realise his vision he had to rely on members of his family and personal friends who gave him active support and accepted heavy responsibility, some of them as almost full time workers. First and foremost was his sister, Marie Louise (1861–1952). She went to the newly opened Sisters' Training Home on the Edgware Road in London in 1888 to help for a short time and stayed for 50 years, during which time she presided over the training of the Sisters and led the women's work of the Society. In spite of her frail physique she left the comfort of a sheltered home for constant hardship and sacrifice. She devoted her whole life to the loyal support of her brother and the work which he established. Her tact and even temper and sometimes her wit helped him through difficult moments. Her only ambitions were to provide the sisters with the best training, to find the most useful openings for them and to support them constantly with her prayers.

From the very beginning of the Church Army one of his closest colleagues was Edward Clifford. Clifford was three years older than Carlile and came from Bristol. After a short business career he became a professional artist. During his training at the Royal Academy in the 1860's he expressed his dislike of 'the many varieties of long hair, dirtiness and dinginess' among his fellow students. His pictures included portraits of General Gordon, Dwight Moody and Father Damien. One of his pictures which hung in Church Army Headquarters for many years depicted members of the Broadlands Conference out of which the Keswick Convention grew. This picture now hangs in the museum at Keswick, and contains the earliest painted portrait of Wilson Carlile.

Carlile and Clifford were both involved in the Moody and Sankey Campaign of 1875 and later Clifford served on the Church Army sub-committee of the Church Parochial Mission Society. When Portcullis Hall opened (see page 29) Clifford was to be seen in Westminster most nights. He wore an artist's cap and a light coloured tweed suit (on which flour showed up less conspicuously when flour bombs were thrown). He frequently carried the big drum, holding it above his head to protect it from knives. He was adept at distracting the attention of the mob to enable Carlile and his other helpers to get on with the preaching. As the Church Army grew he became more and more involved while still earning his living by painting. He made several visits to India to see his brother and to visit missionaries. In 1888—89 he went to Molokai to see for himself the work of Father Damien amongst leprosy sufferers, a work which had always fascinated him. On his return he became the Honorary Evangelistic Secretary of the Church Army, a post which he held until 1904. In 1891 he was admitted by the Bishop of London (Dr. Frederick Temple) as a Diocesan Lay Reader. He lived a strictly disciplined life, with a daily ride on horseback in Hyde Park as his only relaxation. In the evenings he wrote bi-monthly letters to Church Army staff and three collections of these were published under such titles as *A Blue Distance* and *A Green Pasture*, titles very appropriate for an artist's work. The letters written between 1895 and 1906 were very long often running to 30 printed pages full of devotional material, biblical expositions and stories as well as practical advice to the officers.

Another close colleague was Colin F. Campbell who was Honorary Secretary of the Men's Social Department of the Church Army from 1892 to 1910, and a member of the Executive Committee. Campbell lived for most of this time in a Church Army Labour Home, after a discharged prisoner whom he befriended had robbed him of the entire contents of his house during his absence, leaving him only a text of Scripture on a wall. He developed a particular interest in the needs of men who were being discharged from prison and eventually he resigned from the staff of the Church Army to work under the Home Office in connection with discharged prisoners.

In 1917 Mr. F. M. Elgood, C.B.E. (later Sir Frank Elgood) became a Church Army Commissioner on the Western Front and thus began a connection which lasted over 30 years. For most of this time he was a Treasurer of the Society. During the Second World War he was also Chairman of the Board and until Prebendary Treacher's appointment as Head he was also Honorary Central Secretary. His professional knowledge and skill as an architect enabled him to control all the Church Army properties. He inspired the formation of Church Army Housing Ltd in 1924 and was its chairman until shortly before his death in 1948.

Major Thomas Jackson, C.B.E. gave a great deal of his time from 1935 until 1960 to the Men's Social Department and to the provision of housing for large over-crowded families. During the Second World War he was chairman of the committee responsible for the work of the Church Army in the Forces and in Civil Defence.

A number of women of private means devoted most of their time and energy to the work of the Church Army and several of them took charge of one or other of the Departments of the Women's Work and became members of the Board. Miss Nora Hall served in this way from 1899 to 1926. Her particular concerns were for the Night Rescue Work and work amongst barmaids. Miss Evelyn Gay, O.B.E. began her connection with the Church Army in 1893 and soon became the Secretary of the Women's Social Work. She was a close friend of the Carlile family. She pioneered the provision of Church Army Homes for Inebriate Women and Preventive Homes (subsequently known as Training Homes) for young girls. She succeeded Miss Marie Carlile as Head of the Women's Work of the Society. Miss Mary Martindale joined the staff of the Mission Nurses Training Home in 1902 and later as Secretary of the Women's Social Department she was involved in Board and Lodging Homes and in the care of prisoners' families, and participated actively in Church Army work until the Second World War. Miss Janie Walker took charge of various departments beginning in 1908 with the Medical Mission and the

Fresh Air Department which provided holiday homes for needy families and ending with the Motherless Children's Department which she relinquished soon after the end of the second war. Miss M. G. Leech, O.B.E. was of a slightly younger generation and her association with the Church Army lasted from 1914 to 1963. She was a member of the Board for 35 years. She led the women's work of the Church Army and took special interest in the Fresh Air Department.

In 1946 Miss Katharine Inglis, O.B.E. took over the Chairmanship of the Women's Committee and leadership of the Women's Work in succession to Miss Leech. Miss Inglis began her voluntary work with the Church Army in 1934 and quickly took charge of the Sunset Homes and Women's Help Departments. She made a study of the relationship between the voluntary societies and the rapidly developing national social services. Katharine Inglis was the last person who has been able to devote her whole time to Church Army work in a voluntary capacity.

Throughout his sixty years of leadership Wilson Carlile himself served in an honorary capacity as did his sister Marie and so, of course, have all his successors as Chairmen of the Board. Amongst these outstanding service was given by Major General Sir Colin Jardine, C.B., D.S.O., M.C., Lt. General Sir Harold Redman, K.C.B., C.B.E., The Right Reverend F. Evered Lunt, who on one occasion left his hospital bed for a couple of hours to address the Church Army Conference at a critical moment, and the Right Reverend S. W. Betts, C.B.E. who was Chairman for longer than anyone except the Founder. Mrs. Betty Lloyd became Vice Chairman of the Church Army and also of Church Army Housing. She and Jean, Lady Jardine took a very active part in the Moral Welfare (later called Social Care) Department and also in the work of Forces Welfare. Successive Honorary Treasurers, mostly bankers or chartered accountants contributed their skills and knowledge to the management of the Society's finances.

CHAPTER TWO

THE EARLY DAYS – 1882–1892

Militant Evangelism and the need for Social Work

The Church Army was one of a number of movements which arose during the nineteenth century to alleviate the worst evils resulting from the industrial revolution and in particular from urban development. Many of the pioneers of these movements were motivated by Christian principles, and in particular by insights derived directly or indirectly from the Evangelical Revival, and the Oxford Movement. They went into action in various ways. Lord Shaftesbury and others promoted parliamentary legislation to control the employment of children, to improve the conditions of miners, to humanise the care of lunatics and to secure better housing, water supplies, and sanitation in slum areas. Samuel Barnett and many other clergy and laymen, community sisters and women of leisure went to live amongst the poorest people in East and South London, and some established settlements with the aid of University Colleges and Public Schools. Yet others founded societies to deal with specific problems, or to cater for specific needs, e.g. the Y.M.C.A., the Church of England Children's Society, the Church of England Temperance Society. The Christian Socialists were concerned to teach an incarnational theology capable of undermining the systems which perpetuated poverty.

Some of these societies began by simple and direct preaching of the Gospel often in the setting of revival meetings. These societies were of evangelical origin and regarded a right relationship with God as man's basic need. To rouse the masses from indifference it was first of all necessary to attract their attention. Hence the military style, with bands and processions and street-corner preaching. Then to hold their attention indoor meetings and services had to be lively and exciting and full of novelties and surprises.

The best known of the societies which concentrated on personal evangelism is the Salvation Army which came into being in 1865. There is little evidence of any direct connection between the Church Army and the Salvation Army but Wilson Carlile wrote to the *Church Times* in September 1882 about the need for an organisation 'to develop in Church of England work the chief features of the Salvation Army' and he instanced processions, open air meetings, lively services, hymns to secular tunes, testimonies and appeals. In August 1883 the Rev. F. S. Webster wrote in the *Battleaxe* 'The Church Army owes a great debt to the Salvation Army and it is always a pleasure to acknowledge this debt. That great body had proved the value (in reaching the lowest classes) of using badges and processions and of a multitude of short testimonies, and it is our earnest desire that the friendly feeling which exists between the two missions should continue and increase, though there are necessary differences of administration between a society like the Salvation Army and a society like the Church Army.' The main difference was that the Church Army was always loyal to the Anglican Church, and under clerical leadership, however unorthodox its methods of evangelism might seem to be.

One of the men who exercised a very great influence in Wilson Carlile's life was inspired by the example of the Salvation Army. This was the Rev. Evan H. Hopkins, the first Vicar of Holy Trinity, Richmond from 1870—1893. It was at this church that Wilson and Flora Carlile and later Marie Carlile had their first taste of mission work within the Church of England after leaving the Plymouth Brethren. Wilson Carlile wrote of the Rev. Evan Hopkins 'He welcomed me from non-conformity: he afforded me scope for separate mission work: he believed in bringing the worst to the best, and he acted on his belief.' Marie Carlile wrote of him 'He was so wonderful in encouraging us and trusting us each to do our little bit of work in the parish . . . But it was what he taught us of the close Presence of our living Lord that helped us most and enabled some of us, very ordinary and very timid people, to make ventures in the glad life of service.'

In 1881 Hopkins started what he called 'The Church Gospel Army' at Richmond. They built a mission hall holding 700. Rules were drawn up: members were enrolled: the badge was a red cord in the buttonhole. The members attended 'Knee Drill' at 7 on Sunday mornings and took part in an open air meeting at 10 before the morning service. There was a Bible class for men at 3. In the evening there was a procession with band and banner leading to an indoor Gospel meeting with lively singing and personal testimonies. The climax was an after-meeting at which those who wanted to commit themselves to Christ were counselled as they knelt at the 'penitent form'. And so the Church Gospel Army increased.

JOINING FORCES

Evan Hopkins was not the only Anglican to experiment in this way. F. S. Webster an undergraduate whose home was in Richmond started a similar work at St. Aldates, Oxford, where he later became a curate. He called his Corps of lay people 'The Church Salvation Army'. Canon Atherton, Vicar of Bedminster, Bristol, set up what he called a 'Church Mission Army'. When Wilson Carlile decided to leave St. Mary Abbots and develop his mission work on a wider front he consulted with Hopkins, Webster and Atherton and they agreed to combine their forces under the title of 'The Church Army'. A new movement would need some kind of base. At the suggestion of Dr. Carr Glyn, the Vicar of St. Mary Abbots, Wilson Carlile consulted with Canon Wilkinson, Vicar of St. Peter, Eaton Square, and Canon Hay Aitken a noted missioner of the Church Parochial Mission Society. They advised that the Church Army should be established as a branch of that Society, but the advice was not entirely to Carlile's liking. The Church Parochial Mission Society was closely allied with the evangelical wing of the church and Carlile was determined that the Church Army should be as broad and high and deep as the Church herself. His objections were generously met by the Church Parochial Mission Society who appointed a variety of clergy to their committee including Canon Body and Prebendary Shelford. The first governing body of the Church Army was a sub-committee of the Church Parochial Mission Society, consisting of Edward Clifford, Reginald Braithwaite, Dr. Armitage, W. J. Armitage and J. Bowker. This group, with Wilson Carlile as Honorary Chief Secretary, directed the affairs of the Church Army from 1882 to 1885. At first there was little to direct. The Parish Magazine of St. Mary Abbots in July 1882 carried an article expressing appreciation of his work in Kensington and wishing him well in his new work 'of going at the invitation of the incumbents to inaugurate Church lay-work either in connection with or apart from a so-called mission in the parish'. His first task was to sell the idea of working men (and women too were in his mind from the beginning) as lay evangelists. The idea had to be sold to two quite distinct groups of people, viz. likely candidates and clergy who would be willing to employ such evangelists particularly in slum areas.

From the first, Carlile made good use of the Church Press. He wrote of his hopes of providing lay communicants of working class, with some experience of evangelism, for clergy who might wish to use them. The Church papers also carried the first Church Army advertisements for candidates calling for 'Young men . . . full of fire and hard work, ready to give up all for the Lord Jesus'. Applicants must have been surprised at some of the questions included on the form which they received, e.g. 'Can you take a back seat and play "second fiddle" with a happy heart?' 'Can you use the same homely language in speaking for Christ as for your trade?' 'How much indoor and outdoor persecution can you stand without being angry?' 'Can you turn a disturber out of a meeting in a smiling and kindly manner?' 'Have you ever kept an open air meeting going for an hour without one person to help you?'

THE FIRST CORPS

Knowing that example was better than precept he offered to conduct a Church Army Mission in the parish of St. Mark's, Walworth in South London. This involved a nightly procession round the parish led by Carlile with a Church Army Banner. About 50 of his Kensington friends joined him and helped with the singing and brief addresses. They were pelted with rotten eggs and fruit and other handy missiles. Carlile once explained, 'The yolk sticks on the face in a yellow lump, while the white trickles down inside the collar. It wants getting used to!' They succeeded in drawing a number of people into almost equally rowdy meetings in the York Street Mission Hall. In this mission Carlile was joined by W. W. Cox who a few months later became the first Church Army Officer to be commissioned. He opened the first Church Army Station at Richmond and wore the first Church Army uniform made in Bow Lane, London.

From the very beginning Carlile wanted his officers to be parish-based. He saw them as leaders of Corps of local Church Army Soldiers who would get on with open-air witness and indoor evangelism on their own initiative (subject always to the direction of the incumbent). The military language seemed appropriate for Church work which was essentially aggressive, a warfare against sin and ungodliness. One of the early Church Army pamphlets included the following:

'The Church Army is an agency for work outside the Church. Instead of inviting people to come to Church the Army is really the Church going to the people. A Gospel Army without a church is an imperfect organisation, and a Church without an Army is an agency incompetent to reach the masses.'

Before enrolment as a soldier a month's probation was required. A soldier had to be a Church Communicant and a total abstainer who could 'testify clearly to a sense of acceptance with God, and show the reality of conversion in his way of life'. He must also have an earnest zeal for the salvation of souls and be prepared to wear a red cord as a badge of membership and as a sign of willingness to confess Christ openly. Most Corps had a band to provide accompaniment for hymn-singing. They were forbidden to play 'quicksteps sacred or secular' and were expected to confine their repertoire to music which could be sung. A committee minute of 1888 states, 'The Committee would prefer officers to have a few soldiers who could play instruments in spirit as well as in tune rather than encourage a full band'.

Early copies of the *Battleaxe* give news of the activities of the Corps. London, Richmond, Oxford, New Hinksey, Bristol, Tonbridge, Barrow-in-Furness, Exeter, Manchester, Birmingham, Oldham, Brighton, Kings Lynn, Wolverhampton, Lichfield, Norwich, and Swansea are all mentioned in the first six months. The Barrow Corps reported the conversion of a man and wife who had never been inside a church before. At Oxford 'the soldiers march well together and sing as only well-saved churchmen can sing'. At Tonbridge one of the soldiers said that she had 'served the devil for 70 years before she changed masters'. In Cornwall 210 soldiers marched from Pendeen to St. Just 'and the whole town turned out to welcome us'. In Wolverhampton a mission produced 100 adult confirmation candidates.

Corps. of Church Army Soldiers no longer march round parishes with bands and banners. But the Church Army has always associated with it groups of lay people who participate actively in evangelistic work e.g. News Teams, Christian Advance Groups and the Church Army Fellowship.

PORTCULLIS HALL

Wilson Carlile welcomed the opportunity which came to him early in 1883 to have the regular use of Portcullis Hall in Regency Street, Westminster. This was a few hundred yards from Westminster Abbey and the Houses of Parliament. In those days it was a very rough and slummy area, notorious for its number of criminals and prostitutes. It was a place where a continuing mission was urgently needed and which would provide an excellent training situation for the men who were 'drilling' for the Church Army as the cadets in training were then described.

Carlile was also supported by some of his Kensington congregation and by personal friends notably Edward Clifford and Mary Cheshire. Night after night they persisted with open-air processions followed by indoor mission meetings. They would set out with banner, cornet and drum and stop at street corners. They were mercilessly mocked. Red Ochre powder in a pellet of tissue paper was a favourite missile because of its vivid and lasting effect. The banner was a special target because a local publican (who feared that Carlile's influence would be to the detriment of his trade) had offered a free pot of beer for every square inch of the banner brought to him. The Skeleton Army and other hooligans sometimes resorted to violence. Clothing was ripped by razors. Carlile was often physically attacked but he would never prosecute. 'We were a God-send to the roughs of Westminster' said Carlile subsequently. 'They rather shunned other people for fear of police court proceedings but as soon as it got about that nothing of the kind need be feared from us, they used us as bowls and ninepins.' In fact the policy paid off and they had the joy of seeing many of their tormentors converted to Christ.

The climax came on Whit Monday 1883 when an open-air meeting was started in Battersea Park. A gang of roughs showered stones on Carlile and his friends (several of whom were women). Carlile's head and face were badly cut before the roughs desisted. That same evening Carlile set off with a small group of helpers for Portcullis Hall where he was attacked by a man whose brother was in prison for attempting to set fire to the Portcullis Hall. Carlile's injuries revived his spinal weakness and he was incapacitated for six months. Carlile refused to prosecute but was compelled to give evidence. His assailant received a prison sentence but was so much impressed by Carlile's attitude that he became a Christian and later he was involved in active mission work.

When he recovered from his injuries Wilson Carlile travelled widely round England explaining the aims and methods of the Church Army, commending lay evangelism to the church, looking out for suitable candidates for training and encouraging his officers.

The Record describes a Church Army meeting in Oxford in 1884. 'Fine weather, Eights Week, the Australian Cricket Match and College Concerts have combined to reduce work to a minimum. It is almost incredible that any kind of religious meeting held during the week of the races, and at the time of the races could be a success, but the Assembly Room of the Clarendon was packed.'

PUBLICITY

Wilson Carlile continued to make good use of the Church press. His campaigns in Walworth and Westminster and Stepney had already provided good newspaper material and Church papers carried vivid descriptions of the processions with flags and drums and trumpets which enlivened drab areas of the metropolis. Some correspondents, lay and clerical, attacked not only Wilson Carlile's main principle of using relatively untrained men as preachers of the Gospel, but the whole concept of lay ministry. His reply was that the Church Army provides the missing link between the Church and the masses, in the form of itinerant working men trained to reach their fellows with the Gospel. Church Army officers have a mobility which the parish clergy can never have. In the early days Church Army officers rarely stayed in a parish more than a few months. They made a short and sharp impact and then made way for another officer. This prevented any officer from forming a clique, and provided a variety of approach. A further criticism was that a very large number of the early applicants for training, and some of those selected, had strong nonconformist background. Carlile's reply was that many of them had left the Church of England because the Church could not offer them scope for lay preaching and that they were often glad to be back in the Anglican fold. The Church Army has always been a non-party Society and Wilson Carlile discouraged his officers from taking sides in controversial matters of theology and from showing any ecclesiastical party spirit (something he had learned in his curacy at Kensington). In his letters to the press he emphasised that Church Army work in a parish was in every detail under the control of the local incumbent and under the general direction of the Bishop. But his strongest points in press correspondence were always the facts that Church Army soldiers were regular communicant members of the Church of England, and that every year Church Army officers were instrumental in the presentation of large numbers of adult confirmation candidates (2,000 in 1884, 3,000 in 1885) 'mostly gathered from the street corner and public houses'.

Wilson Carlile was not content to rely upon the Church newspapers for his publicity. He launched his own paper. Its original title was *The Battleaxe* or *Gazette of the Church Army Crusaders and Mission Band Movement*. To begin with it was published monthly at 3 Amen Corner, London, E.C. at ½d per copy or 1s 3d post free for a year. The first edition appeared on 2nd April, 1883. Within six months it had proved so popular that publication became fortnightly and from 1884 it was published weekly. In 1886 its title was changed to *The Church Army Gazette*. For its circulation it depended initially on members of the various Church Army Corps. In May 1883 the Richmond Corps sold 1600 copies and the Oxford Corps 1100. Bulk orders were cheaper and the Corps could keep any profits for their own local evangelistic work or for poor relief. In its first year it circulated as far afield as British troops in

India, and for many years the Greater Britain Gazette Brigade sent copies to lonely settlers overseas. Many parishes set up local Gazette Brigades and from the first there was keen competition to see which could sell the most copies. By 1939 the weekly circulation was 120,000, many copies being sold in public houses. There was a trophy presented annually to the Brigade which sold the most. The content of the Gazette included a front page cartoon illustrating some Christian theme, and news of local Church Army activities, as well as directly evangelistic and devotional material. Carlile's first leading article set the tone of the *Gazette*. 'The spirit of aggression must be forced on the Church laity or they will slumber . . . The good parish clergyman is already overworked and the laity must put their hand to the sword. To the soldiers of the Church Army we say "Fire away: tell us how we can help you. The *Battleaxe* is yours, wield it!".' The first editor was the Founder. Subsequent editors included the Rev. F. S. Webster, Miss Mary Cheshire, Miss Mary Burns, Miss L. Thomson, Captain E. Moss and Captain J. A. Dewdney. George Dearmer was Gazette Clerk for 55 years. Publication ceased in 1962 because of increasing costs of production and resulting falls in circulation. The final issue carried on its front page a large cross with the words 'In this sign conquer', an appropriate ending to the publication which was initiated by Wilson Carlile who used to sign himself, 'Yours in the fight'.

The first Conference of Church Army officers and interested clergy was held at Manchester for three days in December 1884. The programme included devotional sessions (two hours of self examination and three hours 'to seek Pentecostal blessing') as well as instruction in methods of evangelism and a public meeting. Wilson Carlile reported a staff of 45 'working men evangelists and between 4000 and 5000 active members many of them at one time drunkards, wife beaters, blasphemers and others — who are now workers in the cause of Christ'.

RECOGNITION BY THE CHURCH

1885 marked an important stage in the development of the Church Army. Early in that year the Church Army became independent of the Church Parochial Mission Society. Whereas in 1883 Wilson Carlile received a very cool and almost hostile reception at the Church Congress in Reading, in 1885 the Church Army appeared on the agenda of the Upper House of the Convocation of Canterbury because Carlile had asked for some kind of licence to be provided for Church Army officers. Strong support came from the Bishops of Oxford, London, Lichfield, Rochester and Truro and the following resolution was approved: 'This house, heartily welcoming the working men who have expressed a desire to serve Christ in His Church and to convert their fellows who have hitherto lived without God in the world, respectfully requests his Grace the President to nominate a committee to report on the existing methods of employing working men for evangelistic purposes'. About the same time the Convocation of York expressed sympathy and interest with the work of the Church Army and gave it every encouragement. And so the Church Army was beginning to find acceptance within the structures of the Church of England. In February 1885 the first Church Army Campaign in Ireland was held in Belfast under the leadership of Captains Davidson and Wine. The second Annual Conference was held this year in London and was attended by 49 officers. The programme included an open-air meeting in Trafalgar Square and a march to Lambeth Palace via the Strand and Whitehall. At Lambeth, Archbishop Benson received the officers and gave them his blessing. The Bishop of Durham (Dr. J. B. Lightfoot) presided at a meeting in Piccadilly and spoke of the 'magnificent hopefulness' of the Church Army officers.

There were various reasons for this change of attitude by the Church. One was the effectiveness of the Church Army in linking adult converts with the church through Confirmation. Another was the loyal adherence of the Church Army to the principle that no Church Army work was started without the approval of the Diocesan Bishop concerned and that the activities of all Captains and their Corps of Soldiers were under the control of the local incumbent. But perhaps the strongest reason was that Wilson Carlile was prepared to modify his methods. He acknowledged that the full Church Army organisation was not suitable in every working class parish and he allowed officers to serve in parishes for short missions or longer periods without building up a corps. Late in 1884 he was prepared in some places to drop the military titles and even the name 'Church Army'. But the Bishops of Oxford and Manchester urged that the name of the Society should be kept.

Not least among the factors which commended the Church Army to the Church at large was the devotion of the Mission Sisters. In 1887 *The Church Army Gazette* carried an 'Important War Notice' inviting women to volunteer for training as Mission Nurses, 'for the conversion of souls and ministering to the sick and afflicted'. Five years later there were 60 Mission Nurses on active service. In the early days careful provision was made to ensure that the nurses were not in a position to exercise authority over men. They were not allowed to lead a procession or conduct an open-air meeting alone, or govern a Church Army Corps. A contemporary commentator wrote as follows: 'A Church Army Mission Nurse has a work which no Church Army Captain could do, still more which neither Rector nor Curate could do, nor even their wives and daughters. She can speak to women, sympathise with them and win their confidence far more successfully than . . . anyone who is above them in education and position both social and official . . . She pays special attention to the sick . . . and conducts Mothers' Meetings, Prayer Meetings, Cottage Meetings and takes an important part in the Sunday School.' The initial basic salary of a Mission Nurse was twelve shillings per week.

One of the first tasks of the Church Army Committee, as well as dealing with day to day matters, was to draw up a constitution for the Society. It was agreed that the Council (i.e. Patrons, Vice-Patrons and General Committee members) should meet annually, the General Committee should meet monthly and a Sub-Committee for Wilson Carlile to consult should meet weekly, a pattern which *mutatis mutandis* has continued throughout the history of the Church Army. The Draft Constitution was formally approved at the 2nd Annual Meeting of the Council in the Jerusalem Chamber in May 1887 and incorporated with the Articles of Association when the Church Army became a limited liability company in 1892.

There was clearly some trouble in Church Army administration quite early in its history. In June 1888 the Annual General Meeting was adjourned for the clarification of certain points by the Central Committee. When it met again in July there was no quorum. Five members of the Central Committee resigned and several new members were appointed, and in 1889 a new President was appointed. (The Earl of Meath succeeded Lord Mount-Temple). In December 1891 there was a proposal to restructure Headquarters and the Rev. J. Chambers, a key member of Headquarters staff since 1886, gave six months notice of resignation. In a private letter dated Christmas Eve 1891 Edward Clifford wrote 'Church Army matters painful and unsettled. Carlile full of beautiful grace'. The cause of the trouble is not recorded in any minutes. There were several controversial matters which combined to put a great strain on Wilson Carlile. Late in 1889 he began the Social Work of the Church Army and this involved raising a great deal of additional income for the Church Army and the burden of this fell largely on Wilson Carlile himself. It is probable that this new venture met with opposition from those who were content for the Church Army to remain the purely evangelistic body which it had been for the first seven years of its existence. Tension of this kind inevitably affected Wilson Carlile's health and to avoid a complete breakdown he was advised to live in the country. Through the good offices of some friends he was offered the living of Netteswell in Essex, where he was Rector for ten months, from March 1891 to January 1892. His country incumbency did not turn out to be a rest-cure. Not only was he frequently in London and travelling round England on Church Army business, but he also threw himself into village life. The church was not centrally situated and so he obtained the use of a barn in the middle of the village and adapted it as a dual-purpose building for clubs and other social activities as well as worship. His stay at Nettlewell opened his eyes to the opportunities for evangelism in country areas and eventually led him to establish a fleet of mobile mission caravans, the first of which was dedicated on 24th June, 1892.

THE BEGINNINGS OF SOCIAL WORK

The year 1889 marked the first important new development in the work of the Church Army. Wilson Carlile regarded it as his 'vocation' to take the Gospel to the people whom he sometimes described as 'the most lost'. His officers were sent to work for the most part in parishes where there was a great deal of poverty and families were living in appalling conditions. Many big towns would provide similar examples of what was written of a London slum area in the 1890's. 'The doors of the houses standing open disclose bare passages and stairways; dirty women congregate on the doorsteps, dirty children play in the gutter and larrikins loaf at the street corners. There is always a good deal of drinking and there is some crime (including murder). The common lodging-houses accommodate the lowest classes, both male and female.'

To talk about the love of God to people living like this, or to men who were homeless and destitute carried little conviction. The Gospel had to be demonstrated in action as well as proclaimed in preaching.

As early as 1886-7 Church Army officers in London, Preston, and one in Australia were supplying free meals for the hungry but this was obviously a method of rendering first aid. Wilson Carlile had been thinking of ways and means of rehabilitating 'honest men in distress' to use a favourite phrase of his. His thinking was stimulated by an account of social work initiated by Pastor von Bodelschwingh in Germany. He saw that the most constructive way of helping men would be to provide them with a setting where they could regain their self respect by helping themselves. And so he planned to provide a home and opportunity for work for men who were prepared to co-operate. His thinking turned into action in the hard winter of 1889-90 when he discovered that men were attending Gospel meetings in a hall in Marylebone because they were cold and ragged and homeless and the mission hall provided a little warmth and comfort for an hour or two before they had to spend the night in the porch or under a railway arch. He invited Captain Shingler to convert part of the mission hall into a simple home for half a dozen men. Captain Shingler wasted no time, 'I at once got hold of two of the men whom we wanted to help, bought some timber and set to work with them to make partitions to form bedrooms, lavatories, a bathroom and a little chapel. We painted and whitewashed all this ourselves and turned the basement into a workshop.' A circular saw was installed and a simple wood chopping industry was started. The home proved popular in spite of its forbidding title 'Tramps' and Inebriates' Labour Home' and soon needed extension. Under the guidance of the Rev. W. H. Hunt, within a year six Labour Homes had been opened on similar lines in London and the Provinces, by 1900 twenty-seven homes were in operation and by 1911 there were 50.

In a letter to the Press in the Autumn of 1890 Carlile wrote as follows: 'We keep the men not less than two months in the home, long enough to constitute a fair moral training against habits of idleness and drink. The place has been more than self supporting as far as food, light and heat are concerned . . . Every morning short prayers take place . . . and in the evening a bright evangelistic march and meeting are held by the corps which uses the same hall . . . In ten months though nineteen have apparently failed and left the Home, twenty-three have been restored to work, respectability and religion and now hold situations from twenty shillings to sixty shillings per week.' The men were paid for the work they did in the Home with deductions for their keep, and were encouraged to deposit a little in a savings fund each week in readiness for the time when they could live independently.

Earlier in the year Carlile had published in *Our Tramps* his plans for a widespread scheme of rehabilitation which included a farm settlement near London where men could be trained in agriculture, and an emigration scheme to the Colonies, both of which came to fruition before the end of the century. It is noteworthy that when General Booth of the Salvation Army published *In Darkest England and the Way Out* his proposals for helping men who had been demoralised by poverty, unemployment and alcohol, were very similar to Carlile's, but on a very much larger scale.

In its Social Work the main policy of the Church Army has been to provide facilities for rehabilitation or other long term help and not merely to give temporary relief. And so many of the Labour Homes soon had Lodging Homes attached to them where single men who had secured regular work could live under more comfortable conditions, until they were ready to fend completely for themselves. One of the problems was to distinguish between the men who genuinely wanted to work and were capable of working, and the scroungers. And so after their first night the men were given a work test. The policy of getting men to do work in return for food and shelter was continued even in the severe conditions of unemployment in London in the years 1903-14 when the Church Army set up emergency night shelters for the homeless and took up lodging-house beds in London. The fee for supper and bed was chopping six baskets of firewood which took about an hour and a half. Carlile was convinced that the best way to deal with the suffering caused by unemployment was 'by enabling the sufferer to earn honest wages, and not by offering gifts which must inevitably end in undermining self-respect and self-reliance, and in turning the unemployed into the unemployable'. King Edward and Queen Alexandra took a personal interest in the relief work of the Church Army. Some of the marquees used in London were known as the King's Labour Tents and some workshops for the employment of married men who were struggling to keep their homes together were known as the Queen's Relief Depots.

The Labour Home pattern was not so successful among women, and a variety of other ways of helping destitute women was devised. Some were cared for in small homes with between 8 and 20 beds. After a time of rehabilitation it was often easy for women and girls to obtain posts as domestic servants, and the Church Army ran a kind of employment agency in London through which several hundreds of women found work each year. Specialised welfare work also developed for women long before similar provision was made for men. As early as 1887, Church Army mission nurses were doing rescue work amongst girls in danger of becoming prostitutes on London streets. Early Church Army Annual Reports refer to Homes for Inebriate Women, Fresh Air Homes for women needing rest and convalescence, and Training Homes for girls.

Before the end of the first decade the general pattern of Church Army work had been hammered out. Its two main branches were the directly evangelistic work and the social work. The development of social work by the Church Army is sometimes regarded as a deviation from its original evangelistic task of winning working class people for Christ. It would however be misleading to regard these as separate divisions, because the over-riding purpose of all the activities of the

Church Army is to make the Gospel of God's love come alive for people. Wilson Carlile was once asked what he would do with a million pounds. He replied: 'I would organise a mission which would be social as well as religious, for I believe that God is as keenly interested in seeing food in the cupboards of the poor and happiness in their homes, as he is in seeing them with Bibles and clean hearts.' He saw the social work as part and parcel of the evangelism, because he was concerned for the needs of the whole person. He was convinced that a man's greatest need was to be made a new creature in Christ, but he saw that poverty and addiction to alcohol could prevent a man from finding Christ. The residential Social Work provided sustained opportunities for direct evangelism, opportunities which were used as far as possible without taking advantage of the predicament in which the residents found themselves. There is no doubt that its development of Social Work made the Church Army acceptable to a much wider public and enabled it to receive financial support from people who were not primarily interested in evangelism. Thus Edward Clifford could tell the Church Congress in 1891, 'A labour home is heartily approved by an average congregation of kindly well meaning people, a congregation often prejudiced against the ordinary mission work of the Church Army'.

The particular ways in which the work developed sometimes appear rather haphazard. This happened because the Founder or one of his staff became aware of some situation where an evangelist was needed or because a specific request for an officer came from some church source, or because some clamant social need forced itself on the attention of the Founder and every endeavour was made to meet such demands. Thus as early as 1883 a few officers went to work abroad. What began as an urban mission soon found itself being extended to country areas. Evangelists were set apart to work with particular groups, e.g. cabmen, or the residents in common lodging houses or the unemployed hanging around the dock gates, or barmaids. As we have seen planning was more evident in the social work. But even in the social work developments were often the result of almost spontaneous response to some obvious need. At a later stage the Head of the Women's Work could write, 'It is natural that changes should constantly be taking place, especially in the Social side of our work where human problems are constantly changing with the changing social pattern. It is a healthy sign of life and growth when such changes in our work are taking place.' It has always been part of the genius of the Church Army to be alive to new needs and to pioneer in meeting those needs, particularly on the spiritual level.

CHAPTER THREE

RAPID EXPANSION – 1892–1902

Urban and Rural Evangelism

At the end of the first ten years there were 180 commissioned Captains in the service of the Church Army and 52 Mission Nurses, but considerably more had been commissioned. For example of the 72 Captains employed by the Church Army in 1885 only 8 were still active in 1892. Of the 24 Mission Nurses employed in 1888 only 6 were still active in 1892. This high rate of turnover declined in the second and subsequent decades. The reasons for the rapid turnover were varied. The work itself was extremely demanding. Officers were highly mobile and were discouraged from putting down roots and this was particularly difficult for men who were married, or wished to marry. Some moved on to work with other Christian Societies and a few became non-conformist ministers. It was not till 1896 that the first Church Army Captain was accepted for ordination in the Church of England. Some of the Mission Nurses left for marriage, others to train as nurses, and a few for service overseas. The main reasons for the decrease in the turnover were the provision of more and more posts in parochial work and in social work where evangelists could stay for much longer periods, and also the more widespread acceptance of Church Army personnel as part of the total ministry of the Church. By the end of the century there were approximately 400 Captains and 200 Mission Nurses on service. Some of these were known as associate officers. They were allowed to remain indefinitely in their posts, but the Church Army did not guarantee to find them work or salary. This arrangement came to an end during the Great War. The basic pay of evangelists at the turn of the century was £1 per week, with small allowances for a wife and up to three children. Mission Nurses were paid eighteen shillings. There was an occasional bonus for long service. Officers equipped with bicycles or tricycles (known as Flying Squadrons on 'chargers') received occasional repair grants. New projects were constantly being brought into operation during the 1890's, coffee taverns providing inexpensive meals, a Church Army Bible Reading Union based on the church lectionary, the Church Army's own printing press, a boat on the Thames for evangelism amongst bargees, the sale of Christian literature by colporteurs, a Church Army Juvenile Brigade, a benevolent fund for officers known as the Church Army Brotherhood, a second-hand clothing department, the enrolment of local secretaries (ordained and lay) to raise money, including some 25 on the continent of Europe (many of whom were recruited by Wilson Carlile on his regular visits to the Riviera). The Annual Report for 1899 describes mission work amongst hop-pickers, fruit pickers, harvesters, in public houses, lodging houses, and no less than 90 workhouses, amongst gypsies, van dwellers, navvies, sailors in Mediterranean ports, at fairs and on race courses. Pioneer missioners in London, Liverpool, Manchester and Leeds were equipped with large tents (which were heated in winter).

This decade saw a number of events which proved to be land marks in Church Army history. We have already mentioned the dedication of the first mission caravan in 1892. This caravan was dedicated at the Marble Arch on St. John the Baptist's Day. At four o'clock the horse was harnessed and set off for the Kent fruit fields. The van carried a letter from Archbishop Benson commending the work to the clergy. The first mission was held at Kidbrooke, near Blackheath. Ten years later there were 68 caravans working mainly in rural areas. This work was supervised by one of the outstanding officers, Captain Philip Prior, who offered himself for training in 1884 after listening to Wilson Carlile at the Church Congress held in Reading in that year. He was the first Church Army officer to be elected to the Board of Management in 1907. After the Great War he became Sub-Warden of the Men's Training Home and led the evangelistic weekends. He was ordained in 1922 and died in 1930. Many stories are told of Philip Prior. One of the best is that a Training Home Prayer Meeting he prayed with great fervour 'Lord, smash the devil' and as he did so he picked up the chair on which he was leaning and brought it down with such force that he smashed the chair.

THE CITY OF LONDON

Wilson Carlile was enticed from his country parish in Essex by the offer of the living of St. Mary-at-Hill in the City of London. This was a church near Billingsgate fish market which like many city churches had no congregation. But Carlile was determined to fill it. His methods were often criticised as being sensational. He installed a magic lantern and threw the whole evening service on to the screen and later on he used cinematograph films. He marched through Billingsgate and City streets with a band which also played for the services. He preached on topical themes like 'The Test Match' or 'The Cup Final' or 'Night Clubs'. The Sunday before Christmas was 'Pudding Sunday' when he asked the congregation to bring plum puddings for the poor. On 'Doll Sunday' he collected toys for poor East End children. The congregation, which was predominantly male, often included professional people, criminals, alcoholics, and homeless men. Carlile gathered round him about a hundred voluntary helpers, and of course he had the support of a few Church Army officers and the cadets in training. As early as 1893 Carlile had a regular Parish Communion on Sunday mornings, with his own sung setting, followed by breakfast. The congregation was then not allowed to disperse, but was marched off to Petticoat Lane for Christian witness and preaching.

Prebendary Carlile, as he became in 1906 when he was given the stall of Newington in St. Paul's Cathedral, retained the living until 1926 when he changed places with his curate the Rev. Captain Robert Halton, so as to devote his time entirely to Church Army work. In the Rectory of St. Mary-at-Hill Carlile set up a City Employment Bureau and Samaritan Office for unemployed clerks and others, where men could be given temporary work while more permanent jobs were sought for them. Several hundreds of men were helped in this way annually. The Church Army presence in the City of London lasted until the second World War. It was restored in a very different form in 1974 when the Rev. H. J. Smith, who had previously been a Church Army Captain and subsequently the Chaplain of the Church Army, became Rector of St. Margaret, Lothbury and used the church and its vestries as a Pastoral Counselling Centre with the assistance of Church Army staff.

PRISON EVANGELISM

In December 1896, the Rev. O. F. Piggott, Chaplain of Wandsworth Prison attended a conference of Church Army officers and was so much impressed by their ministry that he suggested that a Church Army mission should be held inside the prison. The necessary permissions were obtained and in April 1897 Captain William R. Davey began the first Church Army prison mission which lasted for eight days. The result was so satisfactory that the Church Army received permission from the Home Office to conduct an eight day mission in any prison in England and Wales provided that the Governor and Chaplain consented. The missioner preached at a daily service and was available for private interviews. The Church Army Report of 1899 records 'Missions have been conducted during the year in most of the prisons in England and Wales. The simple Gospel has been preached in working men's language; thousands of prisoners have had private interviews in their cells at their own request and practical help has been promised, and given, immediately on their discharge.' In 1900 the Church Army was appointed by the Home Office as a Discharged Prisoners Aid Society. The practical help for homeless discharged offenders was very often the offer of a place in a hostel and assistance with finding a job. The Church Army also set up a Prisoners Families Department, to give financial aid, clothing, holidays and wise counselling to women whose husbands were serving sentences. In 1906, a dozen Church Army Captains and Sisters were appointed as Probation officers. One of the outstanding Prison Missioners of the Church Army was Captain Walter Spencer J.P. who served the Society in various ways for 59 years. From 1911-38 he was Financial Organising Secretary, building up the resources of the Society, but his heart was always in caring for men in prison and helping them on their discharge. From 1911 to the present day a number of Church Army Captains and Sisters have been stationed in prisons as evangelistic assistants to the Chaplains. They take a share in the services and preaching, they often interview prisoners on their arrival, they visit in the cells, and conduct a variety of classes. The most effective evangelism is done in personal conversation when a relationship of trust has been built up.

EMIGRATION

Another development in this period was to arrange emigration facilities for suitable men to go for farming work in Canada. The Church Army provided frequent financial aid for such men and in some cases was able to give them elementary training in agriculture first at a farm in Thelnetham near Diss (the gift of Bishop Wilkinson) and later on an estate of 750 acres at Hempstead Hall in Essex which was acquired in 1905. A few years later the Church Army concentrated its emigration work on boys who found it difficult to obtain employment. They lived for a few months at Stanley House in Stonebridge Park where they learned the elements of horticulture and then moved on to Hempstead Hall for a course in agriculture including the care of animals and poultry, before sailing in the care of a Church Army officer to Canada or Australia. The officer would keep in touch with them and see that they settled successfully. Between 1905 and 1910 the Church Army sponsored 4,573 men and boys for emigration to Canada and only thirty of them were deported back to Britain. To this day there is still a small fund for emigration, but is rarely used.

This decade saw the Diamond Jubilee and death of Queen Victoria and most of the Boer War. Carlile's almost lifelong interest in soldiers led him to offer the War Office free of charge the services of evangelists to assist the Chaplains amongst the British troops in South Africa. Some ten Captains were sent to the front and to hospitals and a dozen others saw active service when they were called up as reservists. It was during this period that the properties in Bryanston Street and the Mews linking them with 12-14 Edgware Road were acquired for use as Headquarters and Training Homes. The total cost of the leasehold sites and the building erected on them appears to have been about £42,000. The new Headquarters was opened in three stages. The Edgware Road section was opened on 1st July, 1904 by Princess Henry of Battenberg and included accommodation for the publication department, a bookshop and visual aids (originally lanterns and slides and later films and film equipment). The main building in Bryanston Street was opened in November 1905 by Princess Louise Augusta of Schleswig-Holstein, and the eastern section by

Princess Christian in April 1908. The official dedication of the buildings was deferred until 1912. These buildings were damaged in the Second World War and continued to be used as the Headquarters of the Society until 1964. The Training Homes were reopened elsewhere after the second war.

THE OFFICE OF EVANGELIST

By the turn of the century Church Army Captains were assured of a recognised place in the lay ministry of the Church of England. In 1896 the Convocation of Canterbury resolved that a trained evangelist should be admitted to the Office of Evangelist by the Bishop of the Diocese in which the Training House is situated and should receive Letters of Admission, after producing:

a A certificate of at least one year's training in a home of which the Bishop as Visitor has approved the rules, forms of service, textbooks and chaplain.

b A certificate that he had satisfied an examiner, appointed by the Bishop, of his proficiency in knowledge of Church Doctrine and of his fitness moral, intellectual and spiritual, for evangelistic work.

c A certificate of godly behaviour from the Head of the Training Home.

To obtain a Bishop's licence or permission the evangelist had to produce his letters of admission, a nomination by a Vicar and a testimonial for the previous year. Evangelists did not normally officiate in consecrated buildings until 1914. Church Army Sisters were recognised as 'Mission Women' but received no official admission to office in the church until 1921, by which time 1,295 women had been commissioned.

CHAPTER FOUR

BALANCED PROGRESS — 1902–1914

Care for the Needy

The third decade in the life of the Church Army was a period of consolidation and steady development in all departments of the work. As has already been seen there was a great deal of unemployment in the early years of the twentieth century. Many men who made their way to London were homeless and destitute, and thousands of them were glad to accept the emergency night shelter which the Church Army (along with other Societies) offered. The year 1905 was a particularly bad year during which more than 350,000 men received temporary residential care in Church Army homes and marquees and over 6,000 of them were able to benefit from a period of rehabilitation lasting for seven or eight months. The Church Army also made a constructive and lasting contribution towards the problems of unemployed men and youths by its emigration scheme. In 1909 the Church Army started what it called City Gardens. It obtained the use of vacant plots of land in Central London and handed them over to married men with families as allotments. For the first year seeds, plants, manure and tools were provided free of charge. Subsequently the man had to cover his expenses by selling produce, as well as supplying his family with vegetables and fruit. The scheme worked well throughout World War I and subsequently. During this period there was close collaboration between the Church Army and the Houseless Poor Society, of which Prebendary Carlile and others were trustees. This Society at one time accommodated over 200 men in five houses.

In 1909 the Church Army acquired a property which stood it in good stead for sixty years. This was the Yorkshire Stingo Brewery in the Marylebone Road, London. The purchase price was £12,000 and a further £10,000 was spent on converting it into a Labour Home (subsequently known as the

Central Welfare Hostel for Men). It was opened by Field
Marshal Lord Roberts in April 1911. It included dormitories
and workshops and a home for first offenders. Special provision was made here for professional men who had fallen on
bad times. During the Great War it was used as a Hostel and
Club for soldiers on leave. During World War II the central
administration of the Church Army was transferred to the
Central Hostel when the Headquarters building in Bryanston
Street was damaged by enemy action. In 1962 the hostel
building was demolished and replaced by a new eight storey
Headquarters Building for the Church Army which was opened
by H.M. the Queen on 3rd December, 1964. Ten years later
when the Church Army was facing a severe financial crisis the
new office block proved to be a valuable asset.

WOMEN'S WORK

Church Army Sisters, as they were now beginning to be
called, were inevitably involved in social care amongst the
poor women and children in the parishes where they were
stationed, as well as in direct evangelism, and a few of them
were qualified midwives. In London there were various special
centres. There was the Barmaids' Rest opened in 1903. It was
open from 8 a.m. till midnight and also provided a few beds.
Barmaids kept very varied hours and needed a club of their
own. The Alexandra Club was opened in the Edgware Road in
1909 as the successor of the Heartsease Club for girls. In the
dining room a good meal was available for a few pence, there
were sitting rooms, a quiet lounge and a number of bedrooms
at six shillings a week for members who needed temporary
accommodation. During the winter educational classes were
held in such subjects as dressmaking, first-aid and singing. The
membership reached the thousand mark, not counting the
junior branch nearby. There was a close link between the
Alexandra Club and the Church Army Holiday Home at
Tankerton throughout the year. The Princess Club in
Bermondsey catered for the needs of factory girls at mid-day
and in the evening. In 1913 some Sisters went to Paris to
care for English girls working in French theatres.
    The Medical Mission of the Church Army in Marylebone
was in its heyday early in this century and continued until

the end of World War II. It was frequented by women and children of families which were too poor to pay a doctor's fee, many of them from the Lisson Grove area. While the patients were waiting a short service was held and after the consultation a cup of tea was served while the prescriptions were being dispensed. A small charge was made for medicine. An evening Bible class was well attended. Many of the mothers who used the medical mission desperately needed a holiday to relieve them of the tensions created by trying to bring up a family in one room without modern facilities. And so the Church Army set up Fresh Air Homes in Bexhill and St. Leonards where a woman with her children could spend a fortnight by the sea and be able to relax for the first time since her marriage. Some of the children suffered from tuberculosis and the Church Army set up a sanatorium for children . at Church Crookham in Hampshire.

AIDS IN EVANGELISM

On the directly evangelistic side there were no significant new ventures in this period, but as the number of Captains and Sisters increased, every department was able to expand. By 1914 there were 70 mission caravans in operation, including at least one in every Diocese of England and Wales (with one exception.) The first Scottish van was opened in 1912. One mission van served gypsies in the New Forest. Seaside missions were developed in the summer holidays at such resorts as Blackpool, Morecambe, Southport, Ramsgate and Southend. There was such a big demand for visual aids that the Lantern Department held a stock of more than 50,000 slides for regular hire and employed a staff to do the necessary art work. In 1910 the Church Army first began to make use of cinematograph films both for evangelism and for publicity about the Society, and soon afterwards obtained its own film equipment, but it was many years before the magic lanterns were replaced by the modern film and filmstrip projectors.

A very important adjunct of most Church Army activities was the printing press. The time came when it was no longer economical to employ printing firms and in 1893 the Church Army had bought its own printing press and set up business in

Salisbury Mews, Marylebone. In 1903, Dr. Ivy Williams, LL.D. gave the Church Army a printing works at Cowley, Oxford, in memory of a deceased relative, initially rent free and subsequently at a rental of £100 per annum. In 1932 she gave the freehold. To begin with the Church Army Press, as it was known, confined its work to the Church Army's own publications. After World War II it printed much ecclesiastical material for the Church Assembly and other bodies, as well as competing in the commercial field. The buildings were extended in 1964 and in 1974 the Church Army Press amalgamated with another printer under the name of Bocardo and Church Army Press.

Wilson Carlile suffered a breakdown in 1907—8 and part of his recuperative period was spent in Ceylon and in the Holy Land, but he recovered in time to attend the Edinburgh World Missionary Conference in 1910. Tensions often affected his health. He strongly disliked majority decisions in committee work and preferred to wait until there was unanimity. Some people interpreted this as his means of getting his own way. There was a lengthy crisis in the Board of the Church Army which came to a head in 1910—11. The details are obscure but the tension was such that it involved an attempt to replace Prebendary Carlile as leader of the Church Army. Archbishop Davidson visited Church Army Headquarters to facilitate a settlement. It concerned the affairs of the Friends of the Poor, which was very closely associated with the Church Army and in which Princess Marie Louise of Schleswig-Holstein took an active part. In 1911 it was decided that the Friends of the Poor (known today as the Friends of the Elderly) should be completely independent of the Church Army. Three board members resigned over the controversy and nine new board members were elected. Shortly afterwards Prebendary Carlile was appointed Permanent Chairman of the Board as long as he remained Honorary Chief Secretary. In 1909 the Rev. Dr. A. E. Richardson joined the staff of the Church Army as Metropolitan Secretary and soon began to take a leading part in its management as Secretary of the Board. In 1913 he was appointed Principal of the Training Home of the Church Army, a position which he held with distinction until 1939.

THE DANISH CHURCH ARMY

In 1912 a Lutheran Danish Church Army came into being. A Danish pastor named Mollerop had spent three years at Hull as a chaplain to seamen and had seen something of the work of the Church Army. He was inspired to establish a similar movement in Denmark. There have been very occasional links with the Church Army in England. Dr. Richardson and the Rev. H. Brewer attended a congress of the Church Army in Denmark in 1934. The Rev. E. W. Carlile paid a visit as Chief Secretary. In 1949 Pastor Hald visited the London Headquarters. A group of Danish officers came to England in 1979 and visited seventeen centres of Church Army work. Today there are about 150 Danish Church Army officers led by Pastor Ole Jensen. Most of them are on the staffs of churches as Evangelists. A few of them work in hostels, in youth clubs, in the care of single parents and in the rehabilitation of drug addicts.

CHAPTER FIVE

THE GREAT WAR – 1914–1918

When the Great War began Wilson Carlile was 67 years old and many people of that age would be thinking of retirement. Wilson Carlile threw himself into the war effort with the vigour of a man in his forties. Nearly half of the Captains and many members of the Headquarters clerical staff enlisted. The Church Army was already well known in the Army and Navy through its barrack room missions. Bishop Taylor Smith, the Chaplain General, welcomed Church Army Captains as lay chaplains.

AT THE FRONT

A Military sub-committee was formed by the Church Army immediately and made plans for the provision of canteens and recreation tents and huts at home and at the front. In a short time a complete war hospital for 105 men was established in a school at Caen, working under the French Red Cross. A dozen of the orderlies were Church Army evangelists, who at least had a first-aid certificate and were able to support the medical and nursing staff and also assisted the chaplains. In 1916 the hospital was transferred to Dungavel in Scotland as a Naval Auxiliary Hospital under the Admiralty. The recreation huts and tents were sometimes named after famous soldiers e.g. the Kitchener Tent in Hyde Park and the Roberts Tent in Woolwich. As well as providing rest recreation and refreshment the centres always afforded chapel facilities with frequent celebrations of Holy Communion and regular evening prayers. Every centre had an evangelist or a clergyman in charge and volunteer staff to help them. The usual pattern of a centre was to have the canteen at one end and the Holy Table at the other, with space for sitting, writing, and amusement in between. The Rev. J. C. V. Duvell, the Chief Com-

missioner of the Church Army in France regarded the Church
Army centres as important factors in the maintenance of
morale among the troops, because they provided not only food
and drink, but also talks, lectures, and discussions which kept
the mind active and spiritual ministry which stimulated and
sustained the whole person. He also made the memorable
comment that 'a liturgical service . . . is much more appreciated than an inorganic sing-song of the kind that men are
popularly supposed to love'.

As the war developed Church Army centres were found in
Malta (20 including one magnificent stone building) Egypt
(200) Gallipoli (20) British East Africa and India (30)
Mesopotamia (30), and later on in Italy and Palestine. By the
end of hostilities about 800 Church Army centres had been in
operation in Europe. Church Army clubs, institutes, and coffee
shops were to be found at all the main Channel Ports, often
on the quays, and also at large railway stations and junctions,
where long delays were experienced. Before the W.A.A.C.s
arrived the Church Army clubs were some of the very few
places where men could have some contact with women, who
staffed canteens not too close to the fighting front. When
necessary the Church Army provided clubs for W.A.A.C.s and
Q.M.A.A.C.s and occasionally arranged joint social functions
for men and women in uniform.

By the spring of 1918 the Church Army had about 200
centres under shell fire on the Western Front. 100 of them
were destroyed in the German advance which began in March
of that year. In the peak period 200,000 men used the centres
every day. The Church Army also provided 50 ambulances and
a number of kitchen cars or mobile canteens which went up
almost into the firing lines, often under cover of darkness. The
first kitchen car served 6,000 hot drinks in its first week and
used over a ton of sugar in its first six months. The centres
supplied notepaper and envelopes free of charge to serving men
and it was calculated that in 1917 about a million sheets of
paper and half a million envelopes were used in this way.

IN GREAT BRITAIN

Great Britain had its share of Church Army canteens and
centres. Some of the men's hostels were adapted to receive

disabled men and for use as clubs by servicemen on leave. 'Charmy' on the Edgware Road, London was opened in February 1918 as a club where service men could entertain their friends of either sex for a meal or games or conversation and attracted up to 2,000 visitors per day. The Hostesses Guild and the Friends of the Wounded cheered many a soldier far from his home and family. In 1917 a house at Tankerton was adapted for convalescent care for 30 men at a time. In London 'Soldiers Welcomes' and 'Soldiers Cabins' supplied refreshments, advice and information. The needs of women were not forgotten. Recreation rooms and a few hostels were opened for women engaged in the manufacture of munitions, and 36 centres were devoted to the care of wives and widows of men on active service. Many thousands of parcels were sent to the trenches and also to prisoners of war (including some of the Russian prisoners in Germany). A typical parcel would contain some food, an article of clothing, and something to read, e.g. a New Testament or a copy of the Soldier's Pocket Companion. The Church Army also escorted wives and mothers of seriously wounded men on visits to French hospitals.

The Church Army maintained as much of the normal peace time work as possible. The men's Training Home was closed. The problems of unemployment no longer existed and so the Labour Homes were adapted for different uses. The Mission Caravans were laid up (with the exception of a very few which were staffed by Sisters). The work in Prisons and amongst discharged prisoners was continued. There was a growing demand for religious lantern slides for evangelistic use and the *Church Army Gazette* had widespread sale. The majority of Church Army Sisters were on the staffs of parishes up and down the land. The need for what was in those days described as Rescue and Preventive work amongst young women and girls was even more urgently needed in wartime. Nearly a thousand residents stayed in the Homes for an average of ten weeks in 1917. In the same year there were about 30 Sisters based in a similar number of towns who had received special training as 'Rescue Workers' and much of their work was done on the streets at night. The Fresh Air Department provided help for many women at risk of breakdown through the pressures of wartime. An offshoot of the Fresh Air work developed in 1916. Church Army Sisters in parishes came across children of soldiers and sailors overseas who were suddenly rendered motherless by the death or serious illness of their mothers. To meet this need four homes were opened for children whose relatives were unable to look after them. This work was extended between the two world wars, for any children whose mothers could not give them the necessary care, and continued until 1958.

An important development of Church Army work in this period was the taking over of the Albion Hill Homes in Brighton for the care of women and girls. This consisted of four separate homes to meet different needs with a detached chapel in the garden. Two reformatories (predecessors of Approved Schools) were opened in 1916–17, one at Southgate, London, and the other at Huyton, Liverpool, both under Home Office inspection, for the care of girls committed by the Courts.

TRAINING THE CHILDREN

The beginnings of Church Army organisations for children can be traced to the wartime period. In 1914 a Church Army Girl Guide Company was formed among the children of women who patronised the 'Old Clo' department and obtained clothes and shoes and household necessities at nominal prices. The first reference to Church Army Scouts dates from 1915, and about the same time the first Better Britain Brigades came into existence. Mary Burn, better known for her work as Editor of the *Church Army Gazette,* borrowed ideas from Scouting and Guiding and added some definite Christian teaching and experimented with groups of children who promised to try to 'leave my country a better place than I found it'. The movement was taken up by a number of Captains and Sisters in parishes up and down England and became more organised in the post war years with over 100 branches and a membership of several thousands. It was discontinued in 1945 when the Church Army entered into active participation in the Scout and Guide Movement.

THE NATIONAL MISSION

Wilson Carlile's activity during the war was widespread. In 1915 he was awarded the Honorary Degree of Doctor of Divinity by the University of Oxford 'in recognition of his services not only to the State in ameliorating the lot of many of the very poorest and in redeeming multitudes of the criminal classes, but also to the Church, by bringing back to the fold vast numbers of those who had strayed away, and in maintaining the office of the Church as first and foremost an evangelising body, with the duty and privilege of preaching the Gospel'. In the winter of 1915—16 he visited the Western Front and insisted on going into danger areas to see conditions for himself. Carlile and his colleagues were already looking forward to the time when hostilities would cease and fresh problems would arise. Towards the end of the war they were already assisting men who had been demobilised because of illness or injury and providing facilities for such men to learn new trades including farming and market gardening. A planning committee was set up to attempt to meet the needs of men who would find it difficult to obtain employment. In 1916 the Church Army gave its active support to the National Mission of Repentance and Hope in which William Temple was the driving force. The Church Army's contribution to the mission was to set aside £2,000 to finance Diocesan 'Flying Squadrons'. These were teams each consisting of two clergy, two laymen and two women (with extra help in large parishes) who would spend the inside of a week in any area to which they were invited to 'arouse the devout but dormant churchfolk to become aggressively militant' in their witness for Christ. Each team was briefly trained by a Church Army officer and went to a fresh parish each day from Tuesday to Friday. They visited from house to house and held short meetings indoors and out of doors. There was no preaching as such, but testimonies to Christ restricted to three minutes. The squadrons visited 555 parishes, more than half of them in the Dioceses of Oxford and Gloucester.

In 1917 the Earl of Meath retired from the office of President of the Church Army after serving in that capacity for 20 years. He was succeeded by the Right Honourable Herbert Pike Pease, P.C., M.P., the Assistant Postmaster-

General (subsequently Lord Daryngton) who had been a member of the Board since 1900. He held the Presidency for 32 years, and so took an active part in Church Army affairs for almost half a century.

The services of the Church Army to the nation were recognised by the appointment of 13 Church Army personnel to one or other of the grades of the Order of the British Empire. The Italian Government honoured three of the staff, including Captain E. Wakefield, with membership of the Order of the Crown of Italy, and three others including Captain Spencer received the 'Medaille du Roi Albert' from the King of the Belgians. The Church Army itself recognised the services of some of its senior officers by allowing them to retain their commission after ordination in 1920. These included Captain A. H. Lloyd, Captain T. W. Thirlwell, Captain C. J. Cottle, Captain P. Prior and Captain R. Halton.

CHAPTER SIX

BETWEEN THE WARS — 1919–1939

The Church Army at Home

As soon as the war was over the Church Army had to address itself to fresh problems. Many of the wartime centres had to continue their work until men were demobilised. In Germany new centres were opened including four in Cologne, and these remained active until 1925. The centre in Ypres was adapted as a hostel for small parties of bereaved people who wanted to visit the graves of men who had been killed. The Church Army also arranged escorts and travel facilities. The Ypres Centre received a series of V.I.P.'s as visitors, including the King of the Belgians, President Wilson, Marshal Foch and General Weygand. In Britain more than 60 of the huts which had been used by troops during the war were adapted as social centres where people could meet and find friends. Each centre had an evangelist in charge. There were always a lounge and a billiard table and canteen facilities. Some centres catered more for the youth of the neighbourhood and provided sporting clubs. Wilson Carlile described the social centre as 'a vigorous antidote to the gin palace'.

The Church Army had to face financial difficulties. The War work had attracted substantial donations as well as bringing income from the sale of refreshments, tobacco, etc. Such income soon began to diminish, because many of those who gave generously for war work were not particularly interested in the normal evangelistic work of the Church Army. A new scale of salaries for Captains and Sisters was introduced because of the growing cost of living. The Church Army had been in existence for nearly forty years and pension provision was beginning to be required. A fund was built up over the years following the War by generous gifts from Prebendary

Carlile's Golden Wedding Fund, and from Mr. W. J. MacAndrew, combined with a substantial earlier bequest from Mrs. Torre and a number of smaller funds which had accumulated over the years for old age provision for the officers. The Torre Pension Fund was finally established in 1928 and remained the sole Church Army pension provision until the 1960's. In 1929 a pension scheme was introduced for the clerical staff at Church Army Headquarters.

EVANGELISTIC CAMPAIGNS

There were also problems of staffing. During the war no men had been trained as officers. 37 evangelists had been killed. Others had joined up and had not returned to the Church Army. Recruits had to be found and the Training Home reopened. The re-deployment of officers after their wartime service was in itself a formidable task. Prebendary Carlile was eager to reopen as much as he could of the directly evangelistic work which had been suspended during the war, but after four years of very different work it was difficult for men to accept, for example, the restrictions of caravan life. However, 25 vans were in operation by 1920 and 50 by 1922, in which year the first motor caravan was used. In 1920 the traditional Church Army summer work was re-started with seaside missions at Blackpool, Morecambe and Cleethorpes, but there was an innovation. Before the peak holiday period a few columns of Marching Crusaders (including a column of Sisters) set off from Sheffield, pulling trek carts, and sleeping in church halls and conducting brief missions mainly in country parishes over the period of about a month. They visited 210 parishes in 1920 before being re-deployed for the seaside missions.

In the following year, when the Training Homes were full again, the summer work was on a much larger scale and over 700 parishes were visited. It was reckoned that half-a-million people heard something of the Gospel message through this crusade. The annual Summer Crusades have gone on ever since with the exception of the period of the Second World War. In recent years the columns have used motor vehicles and so have enabled more time to be given to the actual evangelistic work, and opened up new opportunities which could not have been taken when the limit of a day's journey on foot was about a dozen miles. In 1921 an evangelistic campaign was held in Newport, Monmouthshire, covering 14 parishes simultaneously. The impact of this was so successful that a series of similar campaigns was held over the next few years, including missions in Cheltenham, St. Helens, Wigan, Blackburn, Bootle and Swansea.

A very important event in the history of the Church Army took place in 1921. The Bishop of London agreed to grant Church Army Mission Sisters the same form of certificate as had for long been given to the Captains. 260 Sisters were admitted by the Bishop of Willesden (acting on behalf of the Bishop of London) to the Office of Mission Sister in the Diocese of London. They were not all working in London, but that was the Diocese in which their training had taken place. Thus for the first time Church Army Sisters received formal recognition of their place in the total lay-ministry of the church.

In spite of financial difficulties the Church Army was able to undertake new projects, including a hostel for blind girls in London and a sanatorium for boys aged 12–16 at Farnham in Surrey over which Captain G. P. Barnes presided for many years. Before and after his retirement Captain Barnes kept in touch by correspondence with several hundreds of the boys who had benefited from their time at Farnham. In 1921 the Church Army opened its first Clergy Rest House, to provide holidays for over-worked clergy and their families. This work continued for over half-a-century and indeed at the present day holiday grants are made to clergy in necessitous cases. In 1923 the Church Army organised a weekend Conference on Aggressive Evangelism attended by 32 members of Parochial Church Councils and also some students from Cambridge and St. Bartholomew's Hospital. This proved to be the first of many weekend gatherings at Church Army Headquarters which became known in the Church Army as Evangelistic weekends (E.W.E. for short). The visitors, sometimes as many as a hundred, were lodged in the Training Homes while the Church Army students were away on field-work. They were encouraged to give their testimony at open air meetings at Speakers Corner in Hyde Park (usually in two minutes flat!).

They visited some of the Church Army hostels. They heard brief lectures on evangelism and they were inspired to attempt more active evangelism in their home parishes and places of work.

RENEWED EMIGRATION

As more and more men were demobilised, unemployment once again reached serious proportions. The Church Army work-aid homes were full and in some areas soup kitchens were opened. Many of the social centres attempted to provide occupation for men, to relieve the boredom of enforced idleness. The biggest lasting contribution which the Church Army made in connection with unemployment was through its emigration work which re-opened after the war. Between 1919 and 1929 approximately a thousand persons a year were assisted to emigrate. They went mainly to Canada and Australia, and a few to New Zealand, South Africa and South America. Most were young unmarried men, some were men with wife and family. Applicants were very carefully selected, most of them for their suitability for farm work. After a simple training the emigrants usually travelled in parties conducted by a Church Army officer who remained in the receiving country long enough to make sure that their charges were properly provided for.

In 1920 an agreement was reached between the Church Army and the Council for Social Service of the Church of England in Canada with a view to ensuring the spiritual and material welfare of all Church of England immigrants to Canada. Canon T. Pughe visited Canada to promote the link between the Church Army and the Canadian Church and a special committee was set up in Toronto to plan for the welcoming of the newcomers, and to help them to become good Canadian citizens and churchmen. Early in 1924 Captain and Mrs. Tom Smith went from England to open a Church Army hostel for men in Winnipeg.

Similar arrangements were made with the Church of England authorities in Australia, particularly in the Diocese of Brisbane. Early in 1923 Lt. Col. J. H. Stanley, C.B.E., who had been an Honorary Commissioner of the Church Army in its military work, was appointed as the representative of the Church Army for the purpose of fulfilling its policy of emigration to the Dominions and Colonies of the Empire and immediately he set off for Australia where he worked on much the same lines as Canon Pughe had worked in Canada.

CHURCH ARMY HOUSING

The fourth decade of the Church Army was a period of advance on many fronts. Prebendary Carlile, who was made a Companion of Honour in the New Year Honours in 1926, had long wanted to build houses for large families with low incomes and indeed had considered the problem before the Great War. But the Memorandum and Articles of Association of the Church Army did not permit the building of houses to let. Prebendary Carlile, therefore, set up a Public Utility Society under the name of Church Army Housing Ltd. He kept a large measure of control of the new Society by ensuring that the rules provided for the majority of the Committee of Management to be appointed from among members (in the legal sense) of the Church Army. Mrs. Sowton Barrow of Exmouth gave Prebendary Carlile an initial donation of £500 and said that she would want her money back if a working scheme had not been devised within two months. The Church Army conveyed a third of an acre of market garden at Stonebridge Park to Church Army Housing and early in 1925 six cottages were built on the site and occupied. There were 700 applicants and preference was given to ex-service men with at least five children. Within a year 25 houses were in the course of erection and within two years there were small Church Army Housing estates in Leeds, Swansea, Perth and in the outskirts of Glasgow, as well as several in the London area. In the first five years Church Army Housing built 258 houses. This was the beginning of what was to grow into the largest housing association under the auspices of the Church of England. (See Appendix III).

In this period the Church Army itself acquired properties in London and elsewhere mainly for use as hostels for single homeless persons. Two of these were in the heart of Westminster, very near to where the Church Army had commenced its operations forty years previously. In 1924 the King George's Work-Aid Home was opened in Great Peter

Early Social Work at the rear of the Stingo Brewery

Care of the elderly at Woking, Surrey

Seaside Mission in Boscombe, Dorset

Church Army Hostel in Oxford opened in 1978

Street. After the second World War this was developed into the present King George's Men's Welfare Hostel. Queen Mary Hostel for Women replaced an old lodging house which the Church Army had adapted in 1913. The new hostel was opened by Princess Mary in 1928. In those days it accommodated 150 women who could have bed and bath for 10d per night.

In 1933 a new industrial centre mainly for the steel industry was being set up at Corby in Northamptonshire, and men flocked to it from all parts of the country. But accommodation was very limited. Men slept in garages and barns, in fields and even in the churchyard behind the tombstones. Such beds as there were in lodging houses were often occupied for 23 hours out of the 24 by men on shift work. The Bishop of Peterborough appealed to the Church Army for help and within a month a temporary hostel was set up for 80 men. This was followed later on by the erection of a permanent building in which the Church Army carried on social evangelistic work until it ceased to be financially viable in 1975.

The Church Army participated in the British Empire Exhibition at Wembley in 1924–5 by providing a Rest Room and a stall for the products of the Disabled Men's Industries, and by entertaining lost children until their parents found them. The centrepiece of the Church Army exhibit was an evangelistic caravan which attracted many visitors. This proved to be a good public relations exercise as well as an opportunity for evangelism. Other methods of publicity included a new Church Army Film in 1925, the first Church Army Broadcast Service on 17th October, 1926, the first Church Army appeal on the B.B.C. in 1930 which brought in £1,200, a mobile exhibition which was first used at Oxford in 1929, and a pageant on the theme of the Church Army devised by Miss M. Creagh Henry and produced at the Chelsea Palace Theatre on Prebendary Carlile's 81st birthday and subsequently in tne Provinces.

MOBILISING THE LAITY

Prebendary Carlile's personal involvement in the activities of his army was fantastic for a man of his age. On rare occasions he enjoyed the comforts of home, but for many years when he slept at Headquarters he had a tiny bedroom ten

feet by four with a camp bed, a locker which served as a chair
and a couple of clothes pegs. In 1924 he started regular heal-
ing services at Headquarters. In 1926 he spent six weeks on a
preaching tour in the United States and Canada, helping to
launch the Church Army in the North American Continent.
He met the American President and said prayers at the opening session of the Senate. In 1926–7 he toured England on
what he called the 'World Call Campaign'. He preached in
every cathedral and in many other large churches, evoking the
witness of lay people to Christ. He urged members of the congregation to stand and recite a text of scripture and to renew
their confirmation vows at the Communion rail. These services
lasted up to three hours. It is small wonder that he took ill
early in 1928 and had to rest for six months. The World Call
was not Prebendary Carlile's final word on lay witness. It was
in 1934 when Prebendary Carlile was 87 that he announced
that he was taking on the biggest job of his life, viz 'to open
the mouths of the people in the pews'. He suggested that
teams of lay people within parishes should be trained to take
an active part in local evangelism by visiting from house to
house, by leading house groups, by conducting open air meetings, etc. The groups became known as 'News Teams' because
their chief function was not to preach but to give simple
testimony to the ways in which Jesus Christ was real to them
in daily life. A News Team would sometimes be invited to
visit a neighbouring parish for a special meeting to which non-
churchgoers had been invited.

The writer remembers taking a team from his parish one
night during the Second War to speak in Harrow. There were
several in the team and at a planning meeting the week before
it was agreed that each should speak on a different theme. One
woman spoke on Christ in the home, another on the reality of
prayer, a third on how the Lord had enabled him to put right
a wrong personal relationship. The last speaker was a Churchwarden well over six feet tall who was a wartime fireman. His
theme was how the Lord delivered him from fear. He was
trembling like a leaf at speaking in public about his faith in
Christ. He had never done so before. But to the surprise of
the team he told how on the previous night he had removed
explosives from a burning building. It was certainly red-hot

testimony to the grace of God which enabled him to conquer his fear. The News Team movement took on and at one time there were 500 teams in action, some of whom did regular service among the crowds who sheltered in the London Underground Stations during the war. More than 30 Church Army Captains and Sisters were involved in the training of News Teams under the leadership of Captain Leonard Chidzey.

NINETY PLUS

The News Team movement was Prebendary Carlile's last important innovation, but even at the age of 90 he travelled from his home in Woking to Headquarters four times a week and was actively engaged in the work. His 88th birthday was celebrated by a gathering which included many of his fellow Companions of Honour, the Prebendaries of St. Paul's, and the Members of the Church Army Board. This was held at Wilson Carlile House in Stepney, which was in the course of adaptation into a hostel for 180 homeless men. Money subscribed for his 90th and 91st birthdays was used to build Livingstone House at Stonebridge Park as a new home for 91 young men who had come to London in search of work. His 90th birthday party was attended by the Archbishop of Canterbury (Dr. Lang) and many leaders in the national life, by ex-convicts who had made good and by a policeman who had been on duty at Kensington in 1882 and had protected the young Wilson Carlile from the Skeleton Army. In a brief speech Prebendary Carlile said, 'This is a day of rejoicing for you, but it is a day of humiliation for me. I have been supported by the Archbishop and all the Bishops and by many of the leading men and women. I have been given money for my work. And yet today there are still criminals in this country, still people sleeping out, still people who never say a prayer.' Nevertheless he is on record as saying that life was more worth living at 90 than it was at 19.

In May 1937 Prebendary Carlile was seriously ill but he recovered in time to enjoy the celebrations of the Golden Jubilee of the Women's Work of the Church Army, which culminated in a service in Westminster Abbey in February 1938. Just before the outbreak of the war Miss Marie Carlile retired from the leadership of the Church Army Sisters, after heading up the Women's Work of the Society for fifty years.

Although three senior Sisters had recently been made Deaconesses (A. Benniston, M. Brookfield, and E. A. Ruddle) the time was not yet ripe for a Sister to lead the Women's Work. Miss Evelyn Gay who had worked with the Carliles since 1893 took over the leadership for five years and was succeeded from 1944—1946 by Miss Margaret Leech. The Golden Jubilee of the Men's Social Department in 1939 was overshadowed by the imminence of war, but there was time to celebrate the jubilee at a Garden Party at Fulham Palace when that great friend of Prebendary Carlile and great supporter of the Church Army, Bishop Winnington-Ingram welcomed the Church Army for the last time before his retirement. Captain E. Hanmore, who had been in charge of the Men's Social Department for more than twenty years calculated that in fifty years the Church Army had provided men with a bed for the night and food on 48 million occasions through its residential social work, most of the residents staying for more than one night, except in the emergency shelters.

CHAPTER SEVEN

BETWEEN THE WARS — 1919–1939

The Church Army Overseas

Until the middle 1920's the Church Army was a British based Society, but within a year of its foundation news of the Church Army spread to several parts of the world. In 1883 three Lutheran clergy in Hamburg set up their own short-lived Church Army. Requests came in from various places for the loan of Church Army Captains. In October 1883 Captain Thomas Nickless and Lieutenant Cross were seconded for work in the U.S.A. In 1885 the Church Army Committee received a request to send officers to Sydney. The Committee minute reads as follows: 'We will send forth some of the ablest men we have. We cannot spare them, but we trust the Great Divine Commander of the Church Army to send us other and better men in their places.' And so in January 1886 Captain Healey set off for Australia accompanied by another 'intelligent officer' whose name the minute book does not record. Later in 1886 Captains Robertson, Eccleston, Winfield, Howcroft and Munns were despatched to Canada. In 1887–8 Captains Allison, Jessop, Perry and Rhodes went to India, to Calcutta, Amritsar and Santalia. A few years later Mission Nurses Hill and Bennett went to Lucknow where the Bishop was the brother of Edward Clifford. In 1887 Captains Rogers and Murray went to the U.S.A. In 1889 the Committee seriously considered responding to an invitation to send officers to China, but did not in fact do so. From time to time other officers went abroad and some of them took the logical step of transferring to overseas missionary societies.

ACROSS THE ATLANTIC

It was not until after the Great War that the opportunity arose for the establishment of the Church Army as an autonomous society in other parts of the world. Lt. Col. Stanley visited Canada in 1924 in connection with the emigration work of the Church Army and extended his trip into the United States. There he made contact with some of the American Bishops, who suggested that the Church Army might send a group of officers to conduct lay evangelistic work in America. The result was that on 22nd May, 1925, 23 Church Army officers arrived in New York to join Captain Frank Mountford and Captain Arthur Casey who had been preparing the way for a tour of Evangelistic Witness in the Eastern States. The tour lasted for four months and was followed by a similar tour in 1926 in which, as we have seen, Prebendary Carlile took a leading part. In March 1926 Prebendary Carlile wrote to the Bishop of New York as follows:

'I think it is the considered opinion of yourself and others that something on Church Army lines might be started. My prayer and hope is that we may be able to find and enthuse some one pivotal man to give up good prospects in order to work amongst those who are not touched by the ordinary ministrations of the Church and to draw them in. Any counsel or help we could give from our Central Headquarters would gladly be at your disposal. The Column visiting U.S.A. and the one proceeding to Canada are fair samples of the thousand paid workers we have on our Staff, who have gladly forsaken good chances of making money in order to share with Christ the joy of making *men*. They are honest humble men of God.

We come to thank America for the splendid help of such men as Bishop Phillips Brooks, Bishop Brent, yourself and others: also for Mr. Moody, Mr. Sankey and Mrs. Hannah Whitall Smith to whom I personally owe a great debt. It was Mr. Moody who led more to become clergymen, including myself, in England than anyone else of his day. We thank God for America's noble lead for righteousness.

It was a real delight during the War to welcome your brave men in our huts and dugouts on the fighting front.

My sister who comes with me has trained over a thousand devoted, modest and pushing evangelistic C.A. Sisters whose ministry is being richly blessed. A column of seven Sisters will be going to Montreal.

Though I am in my 80th year I am still a learner and hope to get from America many new and useful lines of action, and whiffs of fresh inspiration from your up-to-date methods.'

In December 1927 the Church Army in the United States came into being with Samuel Thorne as its first president. Captain Mountford remained in America and led the Church Army until 1939 when Captain Esterbrook took charge. The Headquarters was in New York and the Training Centre at Providence, Rhode Island. Candidates responded to a call for 'Young men of culture and consecration to dedicate their gifts and manhood for a space of years to real, right down, sane evangelism . . . Toilers, Thinkers, Artisan or Collegiate would be welcome'. The first group of students entered training in January 1928. Early developments were caravan work in rural areas, camps for boys, and lay training sessions known as 'Pew Power Clinics'. Two American officers attended the English Church Army Conference in May 1929, and Captain Davey attended the first Church Army Conference in America in 1930 when 27 Captains and Cadets were mustered.

CANADA

In Canada the Church Army was already known through its emigration work and also because there had been a society called the Church Army at work in the Diocese of Caledonia for many years. About 1896 Archdeacon Collison who had seen the Church Army at work in England introduced its methods of lay evangelism amongst the Indian communities in British Columbia with considerable success. In several places, notably in the Queen Charlotte Islands, Church Army Corps have maintained consistent lay witness for eighty years. They have had very little contact with the official Church Army in Canada, but they work closely with the local church and conduct their own services usually in the Indian tongue. And so when Captain Casey arrived in 1925 and 1926 with a team which in the latter year consisted of 12 Captains and 8 Sisters there was a ready welcome wherever they went. In 1928 another team visited every parish in the Diocese of Huron. The Church Army in Canada was launched in 1929, when a training centre was opened in Toronto and during the summer the first group of students marched from Toronto to Ottawa. The Society was formally inaugurated in February 1930 under the leadership of Captain A. Casey, who was followed as leader by Captain Lennox in 1936.

ASIA

Between 1925 and 1935 requests for the help of Church Army officers came from India, China, Japan, Tanganyika, South Africa, Hawaii, the West Indies and South America, and in most cases there was a positive response. Amongst those who went to India in this period were Sisters Easton, Gowen, Irvine, Stanton and Ward, Captains Hayne and Taylor (Dornakal) Foxcroft and Arthur Shaw (Santalia) Marrison and Weaver (Central Provinces). Captains S. Sherwood and W. T. Jenkins and Sisters L. Whitworth and Parker served in Western China. Captains Baker and Gilligan went to the Diocese of Kyushu. Captains Benson, Roberts and Oliphant spent several years in the Hawaian Islands and Captains Harding and Marsden worked in South Africa. None of these links with other countries led directly to the establishment of local Church Army Societies.

At one time it looked as if an Indian Church Army would be formed. Bishop Azariah of Dornakal visited England in 1926 and took back with him four Church Army officers for his own diocese. It was his intention these should by the quality of their evangelism commend Church Army methods and attract Indians for training, but the Bishop's enthusiasm was not shared by other Indian bishops and so the scheme never came to fruition. One of the four officers who went to Dornakal was Captain Philip Hayne who returned to England after World War II. He was so deeply convinced that in due course he would be called back to India that he kept up the local language (Telugu) in conversation with his wife for sixteen years. At the end of that time a donation was received by the New Zealand C.M.S. to pay for a missionary on Captain Hayne's old mission station, and so he was re-appointed at the age of 64 and completed his overseas service as a Presbyter of the Church of South India.

Captain Arthur Malcolm and some Australian Aborigines

Conference of Church Army Leaders, 1976
Front row, left to right — Sister E. Carr (Deputy Chief Secretary in England);
Prebendary D. M. Lynch (England); Sister Norma Thompson (Belize); Rev.
Michael Turnbull (England); Rev. Crispus Nzano (East Africa); *Back row, left
to right* — Sister L. R. Thrush (East Africa); Captain R. L. Gwilt (Australia);
Captain W. Paddock (U.S.A.); Captain J. Dewdney (New Zealand); Captain
R. A. Taylor (Canada); Captain E. Cousins (Jamaica); Captain J. Ball (East Africa)

Roy Heasman House at Beckenham, Kent, for very young single
mothers and their babies

Youth work at Granville House in Birmingham

AUSTRALASIA

The establishment of autonomous Church Armies in the U.S.A. and Canada was followed in the 1930's by similar moves in Australia and New Zealand. Australian Bishops who attended the Lambeth Conference in 1930 were impressed by what they saw and heard of the Church Army and asked for a team of officers to be sent to Australia to conduct a series of missions throughout the Commonwealth. In May 1931 six Captains and two Sisters sailed for Australia led by Captain J. S. Cowland. Captain Cowland reported at the English Church Army Conference in 1934 that 25 Bishops were sponsoring the formation of an Australian Church Army and that funds were coming in to establish a Training College. Donations included a farm and a caravan for Tasmania. They were already looking forward to a ministry amongst aborigines, including leprosy sufferers. For 25 years the Australian Church Army was based at Newcastle and in 1961–2 the Headquarters and Training College moved into the suburbs of Sydney.

As early as 1912 a New Zealand Bishop had suggested that Church Army candidates from New Zealand should be trained in England and the English Board had offered to send an officer to develop Church Army work in New Zealand. Then came the war and the idea was not revived until 1931. Occasionally English Captains had worked in New Zealand, mainly in the Waiapu Diocese, amongst men engaged in railway construction. Captains B. Ball, H. Squires and R. J. Kirby and Wright assisted with earthquake relief in 1931 and a social centre was opened at Napier. As a result of this and of meeting the Church Army at the Lambeth Conference the Archbishop of New Zealand asked for the loan of a team of officers as a kind of advance party. In April 1933 Captain Stanley R. Banyard sailed for New Zealand to prepare the way for a column of eight Captains and two Sisters who set sail two months later. The team was led by Captain E. E. Beck and in the course of two years held missions in every diocese. In 1934 the General Synod expressed the hope that a New Zealand branch of the Church Army would be formed and on 4th March, 1935 the Society was officially founded as an autonomous body with Headquarters and Training College in Auckland. The first Dominion Director was Captain Banyard.

The first New Zealand Captain to be commissioned in 1936 was Captain C. D. C. Caswell, who later as Canon Caswell was Chairman of the Church Army Board. The main credit for the firm establishment of the Church Army in New Zealand must be given to Captain Banyard who combined the qualities of indefatigable faith, boundless energy, and an exceptional organising ability with a heart of compassion. He led the New Zealand Church Army for fifteen years and then devoted himself to the care of prisoners before and after their discharge.

TANGANYIKA

There were two other areas in which the Church Army was active in the 1930's and where many years later autonomous Church Armies came into being, viz. East Africa and the Caribbean. The work in East Africa began as a typical piece of missionary outreach. Captain Frank Shaw responded to an invitation from the Bishop of Central Tanganyika in 1930 to undertake primary evangelism. He was followed in 1933 by Captains J. Bennett and F. Geikie. Captain Geikie wrote, 'Here I am at last in my parish 200 miles long, inhabited by some 200,000 people, who for the most part have never yet heard the name of the Lord Jesus'. Captain Varley, Sister L. Thrush and Sister K. Perry (subsequently Mrs. Geikie) sailed in October 1934, and Captain and Mrs. Jenkins and Sister F. Carter followed in 1935. At one stage there were fifteen officers serving in Tanganyika, several of them in the far west of the country. Their work included medical care and teaching as well as evangelism. Captain Bennett, O.B.E. made an outstanding contribution in the life of the church and the nation by training evangelists and teachers and later by serving as a member of the Legislative Council.

THE CARIBBEAN

In the Caribbean the Church Army has been known since about 1900, when a clergyman introduced the idea of Church Army Corps in parishes in Barbados. They have never had any trained officers, but fifty years later 25 battalions were actively engaged in open air services, prayer meetings and sick visiting. Each group elects its own Captain and Lieutenants, rather on the same pattern as the Church Army in the Canadian Diocese of Caledonia.

From time to time one or two Church Army officers have found their way to Jamaica since 1892, among them Sister Clarke who arrived in 1928 and resigned in 1932 on her marriage to the Rev. H. S. Lynch. She was replaced by Captain W. S. Smith. At one time it looked as if a Church Army might be formed in Trinidad. In 1934 Captain C. R. Williams arrived for evangelistic work and also to represent the Bishop in the Courts of the Colony and to serve as a probation officer for Anglican young people who were in trouble with the police. He was also responsible for setting up an orphanage and an industrial school, and became Honorary Assistant Superintendent of prisons. As his work increased four other Captains were drafted to Trinidad Captains F. Marsden, Allen, Cooper and Silman. Captain and Mrs. Silman had previously been working in British Honduras. In 1943 the Bishop of Trinidad ordained Captain Williams. Church Army Headquarters recalled the remaining officers to Headquarters, but in wartime travel was impossible and so Captains Allen, Cooper and Silman accepted ordination and remained in Trinidad. Then the only Church Army presence in Trinidad consisted of three indigenous men to whom Captain Williams had given a little training.

Behind all this overseas development was the watchful eye of Captain W. R. Davey, O.B.E., who joined Headquarters Staff before the Great War and somehow managed to hold together the unlikely combination of being Secretary at the same time of the Sisters' Parochial Department and the Prisons and Workhouse Mission Departments. His main work in the Society between the wars was to direct all the short missions including caravans, pioneer missions, summer crusades and prison missions and to supervise the work overseas in so far as that was possible. He and his close colleague Captain Bird both toured many of the places where the officers were serving abroad. It was his ambition that the Church Army should be established as a local Society in all the countries where its missionaries were stationed. He completed fifty years of active service in the Church Army in 1940.

CHAPTER EIGHT

WORLD WAR II AND ITS AFTERMATH
1939–1950

Prebendary Carlile was in his 93rd year when war came again. He continued to travel frequently to London but it soon became obvious that younger and more vigorous leadership was necessary and no one was more aware of this than the Chief himself. In November 1939 Mr. Frank Elgood undertook the duties of Honorary Central Secretary as well as being Honorary Treasurer and Controller of Church Army properties and Chairman of Church Army Housing. This relieved Prebendary Carlile of much responsibility but it could be only a temporary arrangement. In December 1941 the Board was informed that the President (Lord Daryngton) had talked with the Chief and with the Archbishop of Canterbury (Dr. Lang) about the future leadership of the Society. In January 1942, a few days before the Chief's 95th birthday, a further meeting was held at which six officers were also present and it was agreed to look for an ordained or lay man to take charge of the Society's affairs. He should wear the uniform and keep the Officers' Rule of Life. A few days later Mr. Elgood was elected Chairman of the Board.

PREBENDARY TREACHER

To follow the man who had founded the Church Army and led it for sixty years was a daunting task for anyone and it is small wonder that two clergymen (one a future bishop) refused the offer of the leadership. It was on June 26th that Prebendary Carlile himself proposed to the Board that the Reverend Hubert Harold Treacher, Rector of Hanley and Rural Dean of Stoke-on-Trent, should be appointed leader of the Church Army with the title of General Secretary and Head. It was agreed that his appointment should date from the middle of September and plans were made for a Commissioning Service to be held in Westminster Abbey on October 2nd. Mr. Treacher took up his duties on Monday, September 21st. On Thursday, September 24th, Prebendary Carlile visited a sick neighbour in Woking and later that evening he fell and lapsed into unconsciousness. He died on Saturday, September 26th. His brother Sir Hildred Carlile died at the age of 90 on the same day. The Archbishop of Canterbury was Chairman of a meeting in the Albert Hall that evening and he asked the audience to stand in memory of one who had done 'more than anyone else in the last two generations to bring the Gospel of Christ in living force to bear upon the people of this land'. His funeral was held in St. Paul's Cathedral on October 2nd and he was buried in the Crypt. The Church Army observes his birthday, January 14th, as Founder's Day with a service in the Crypt of St. Paul's.

The Reverend Hubert Treacher brought to the Church Army a varied experience as a fitter and turner in Chatham Dockyard, and as an Army officer serving in France, Singapore, India and Mesopotamia. He was ordained in 1920 and served as curate and vicar in several Medway parishes before being appointed Rector of Hanley. He was commissioned as Head of the Church Army by Archbishop Temple in Westminster Abbey on 3rd November, 1942. He brought to the Church Army a wide knowledge of people and a genius for friendship. He knew little about the Church Army on his appointment and Captain Pickering was attached to him initially as his aide. He threw himself into his new work with great energy and enthusiasm, travelling constantly round England, visiting and encouraging the Church Army officers. Unfortunately he was dogged by ill health and resigned after seven years. But in those seven years he was able to see through some of the changes which were necessary to enable the Church Army to adapt itself to the post war situation. He became a Prebendary of St. Paul's and a Chaplain to the King.

WAR WORK IN BRITAIN

Early in 1939 the Church Army set up a Committee under the Chairmanship of Major Thomas Jackson, to consider what the Church Army should do in the event of war and how its evangelistic and welfare resources could be used and expanded. Plans were made to adapt Church Army hostels and social centres for the use of men and women in the services, and to set up new centres in places where there were concentrations of troops. In June 1939 several evangelists were detailed to assist Chaplains at Aldershot and elsewhere. By August 1939 recreation centres had already been opened in Taunton, Cranfield, Wokingham, Fleet and Aldershot. As soon as war was declared the Church Army War Committee met daily to administer the affairs of the War Work Department. Captain A. Casey was appointed Organising Secretary and his staff included Captains Howlett, Gearing, Chidzey and Gardham. Major Jackson represented the Church Army on the Council of Voluntary War Work which co-ordinated the welfare activities of the Salvation Army, Y.M.C.A., Toc H. etc. The Church Army's own war work became so extensive that four separate committees were set up to administer the huts and caravans, the hostels and mobile canteens, the welfare facilities for women in the Services and the personnel for the whole exercise. It was agreed at the start that Church Army Captains should not be registered as Ministers of Religion but that exemption from military service should be applied for in each case. The Men's Training College remained open for six months after war broke out, to enable those who were in training to complete their course before going overseas in Church Army canteens. The training of Sisters continued under war time difficulties and altogether 80 were commissioned between 1939 and 1945. Many of the Sisters who worked in parishes were involved in the problems of the evacuation of children from danger areas, in caring for the bereaved, and helping the homeless when 'incidents' had occurred.

The Military Huts Committee of the Church Army supervised recreation huts and canteens for men and women in all the Services at home and abroad, staffed very largely by voluntary workers. The volume of the work involved in Britain varied from local canteens like that in Gravesend with perhaps 500 customers a day, to those on big railway stations like Crewe where 25,000 meals and 30,000 sandwiches might be served in a week with a 24-hour service. The Taunton Station Canteen in 1940 received warning that French and Belgian troops evacuated from Dunkirk would be arriving. In two days the team of fifty volunteers served 25,000 buns and 10,000 cups of tea and coffee besides many other food items. The huts provided for the spiritual needs of men. There was usually a chapel or at least a quiet room with regular prayers. Chaplains and local clergy often celebrated the Holy Communion. Cardiff reported a typical hut of routine service, 'In one week 13,000 men and women were served, 80 gospels were distributed, two services were held, 250 letters on Church Army notepaper were posted, 91 men slept in the hut free of charge and 70 more were put up by various members of the voluntary staff, while three entertainments were given during the week'.

Men and women passing through London and other large cities needed temporary accommodation on their way home or for a day or two's rest. The Church Army adapted its hostels for this purpose and opened several new hostels to meet this need. Two magnificent houses in Bryanston Square in London were adapted into hostels, each with 150 beds where men and women could stay for a shilling a night. A hostel in Paddington was used by many soldiers travelling to and from the West Country in the early part of the war. When it was destroyed by enemy action Captain W. Bailey was awarded the George Medal for his bravery.

Church Army mobile canteens operated in many parts of Britain amongst civilians as well as men and women in all the Services. Sixty canteens were on the road within the first year. Canteens were often on the spot within an hour of a bomb explosion during the 'blitz', bringing refreshment for homeless people, firemen and civil defence workers in London, Norwich, Coventry, Hull, Sheffield, and many other towns. The mobile canteens were specially appreciated by men and women on isolated gun sites, not only because they brought a change of diet, toilet requisites, aspirins and cosmetics, but because it meant personal touch with the outside world. Air fields, ports of embarkation, dockyards, training grounds were frequently visited. There were a few mobile libraries and cinemas and one mobile social room complete with projector, piano and a stage, which like many of the ordinary mobiles was supplied by America.

Some of the Church Army's most important war work was done in air-raid shelters, where many services were held. In London this was on a large scale, particularly on Underground Railway Stations where thousands of people slept every night on the platforms. In 1940 Captain L. W. Chidzey obtained permission for the Church Army to hold services of up to 20 minutes' duration and similar permission was given to the Salvation Army. The opportunity for Christian witness was enormous. The Church Army seconded only eight officers. Captain Chidzey consulted with local clergy near the stations and 100 teams of volunteers from various denominations covered 80 stations regularly. A team might take as many as eight little services during an evening. They were very simple, including two or three popular hymns accompanied by a piano accordion, a very brief address or testimony, and a prayer. Near Liverpool Street Station part of a disused line was converted into a shelter where thousands of people slept in bunks. Here the Church Army had the use of a large hall with stage, piano and microphone, and several hundreds of people often took part in the services. Confirmation classes were held in some of the shelters. The largest shelter of all was in the Chislehurst Caves which extend for miles, and became 'home' for about 25,000 people, many of whom had lost their houses through bombing. This became a real evangelistic and social welfare centre. A large hall served as church, concert hall, and community centre.

AT THE FRONTS

The Church Army was ready to go to France as soon as permission was given and in December 1939 Captain Ayrton opened a canteen at Boulogne, and in January 1940 Captain Chippington started a canteen near the railway station at Arras. This was often open from 8 a.m. until 2 a.m. the next day. The facilities included a games room and a Chapel as well as the canteen. By mid-May a dozen Church Army Centres were open in France, but of course they were all lost along with three mobile canteens, in the German advance. All the Church Army staff escaped, except for two clergymen who stayed with the wounded soldiers and were captured. They were both repatriated in 1943.

Three Church Army Sisters working in Rouen escaped on the last boat out of St. Malo. Two more working at Nantes escaped via St. Nazaire on the *Lancastrian* which was sunk. They were thrown into the sea and rescued by one of the ship's boats and were twice machine gunned and eventually were rescued by a French trawler. Frank Casey (brother of Captain A. Casey) escaped on the *Floriston* from St. Nazaire. The ship survived two air attacks and three submarine attacks and brought 3,600 men safely to Plymouth.

Frank Casey's next assignment was to organise Church Army Welfare Work amongst the British Forces in the Middle East, where he was shortly joined by Captain George Gardner. Their initial equipment was one mobile canteen, an excellent Ford vehicle with gas for cooking, ice boxes, and a large tank capable of holding a ton of water. Three more of these vehicles were immediately put on order, and well used during the desert campaign, often very close to the action. But just as important as supporting the men at the front was the provision of leisure facilities for the many thousands of men of the Allied Forces at the base stations who were often bored and had nowhere to go for local leave.

In January 1941 sites were secured for a large hut at the convalescent depot at Nathanya in Palestine, and for centres at Suez, Sholoufa and Kantara in Egypt. One of the most popular centres was known as the 'Pig and Whistle', on one of the few bathing beaches available to the Army. Mobile canteens frequently visited isolated units in Egypt and the Sudan and were involved in the campaign in Eritrea and Ethiopia penetrating as far as Gondar and Addis Ababa. A permanent Church Army Club was opened in Asmara in a building where Mussolini had lived. Captain Reeman took a mobile canteen to Iran to assist the men of the 6th Indian Division. In Iraq there were two mobiles and clubs in Mosul, Baghdad and Sheibah.

A little welfare work was done by Church Army Staff in India. Captain and Mrs. Marrison ran a canteen in Nagpur. Captain and Mrs. Hayne travelled many miles with a vehicle which combined a library, a shop and a tea-bar. Captain Gearing who held a commission in the Royal Artillery was released to run a canteen at Katni.

In September 1941 a hostel was opened in Damascus where nearly fifty men could stay on leave at reasonable prices. In November 1942 a similar hostel was opened in Jerusalem. Sister Chamley and other Church Army Staff escorted hundreds of service men and women to the sacred sites in and around the city. The hostel also housed refresher courses for chaplains and gave hospitality to ordination candidates, so that they could have a preliminary course while still in uniform. In March 1943 a large club was opened in Alexandria with a tea garden, lecture rooms, a hall and a dining room.

As the British Forces moved across North Africa more mobile canteens were pressed into service. One centre was opened at Derna in Libya and four centres in Tripoli including the National Hotel and the Rialto Restaurant.

Sister Guest, Sister E. Thrush, Captain Cox and Mr. Herbert Croyden arrived in Algiers in April 1943 and worked with the French Red Cross before moving into Italy early in 1944. Captain Gardner left Egypt early in 1943 to co-ordinate Church Army work in North Africa and as soon as British troops moved into Sicily and Italy he became Church Army Commissioner for the whole of the Central Mediterranean. His main tasks were to deploy to the best advantage the two dozen Church Army staff who were available and to maintain supplies. Mobile canteens were at Anzio and Cassino, moving as near the front as possible, often under cover of darkness, bringing tea and cakes to men in the fighting line. D. H. Barber wrote, 'What Italy was like at times can be imagined when many of the troops looked back with nostalgia to the "good old desert" where they had been merely choked with dust instead of drenched and frozen'. As the front moved northwards the Church Army established large centres where men could relax in comfort, at Naples, Salerno, Siena, Pescara, Pontecagno, Cesenatico, and ultimately in Milan in 1945. The Centre in Naples was a five storey building. The cafeteria on the ground floor served about 4,000 men a day. Above were lounges, writing rooms, a barber's shop, a tailoring establishment and two floors of bedrooms which could accommodate 150 men. The Centre in Milan was equally palatial, with restaurants and a ballroom. During the period of preparation for demobilisation about 5,000 men used the centre daily, and consumed a hundred urns of tea and coffee. A staff of 100 Italians was employed. About 1,500 doughnuts and 3,000 cakes were made and sold on the premises each day. Mr. H. Croyden was able to leave a substantial credit balance when he closed the Centre and wound up the Church Army's affairs in Italy in 1946.

With the invasion of Normandy on 'D' Day came many new opportunities of service first for the mobile canteens and later for centres and hostels. Customers included a group of R.A.F. men who had been shot down and harboured in French villages for months. By the end of 1944 there were 18 Church Army mobiles and eleven static centres in North-West Europe. D. H. Barber writes, 'Brussels Hostel was going strong, but the beds captured from the Germans were of poor quality and annoyed Captain Bucknell intensely as he thought they would get the Church Army a bad name'. One convoy of Church Army vehicles took food, blankets, clothing and medical supplies to villages in the Ardennes in severe winter weather. A mobile canteen waited for men of the 1st Airborne Division at Nijmegen on their return from Arnhem. Captain H. J. Smith (subsequently Chaplain and Director of Counselling in the Church Army) and his wife Peggy were in charge of a canteen which had the curious description of 'Mobile Static'. It consisted of two lorry loads of equipment which moved forward into a series of requisitioned buildings as the front advanced. Mrs. Smith was the first British woman to get into Germany during the war. After VE Day canteens and hostels were set up in Germany, including clubs at Hamburg, Dusseldorf and Gatow near Berlin.

The work of the Church Army in Germany has continued to the present day amongst the personnel of the B.A.O.R. under the direction of a series of Senior Representatives, in which capacity Mr. Croyden served for two periods. It was particularly successful during the days when many young National Service men were stationed in Germany. Today the work is mainly among the families of the soldiers, and is appreciated by the women when their husbands are on duty in Northern Ireland.

This account of the work of the Church Army amongst
H.M. Forces would not be complete without a record of the
spiritual work which Church Army evangelists and clergy were
enabled to do through the various centres. Most of the centres
had a chapel with regular daily prayers. On special occasions
hundreds of men would gather voluntarily for worship. It was
a common sight to see men dropping in to a chapel or quiet
room for a moment of private prayer or thanksgiving. Services
were held in military hospitals, on remote gun-sites, in a shack
of sandbags and petrol tins on the Anzio beach head, in the
hold of a Greek ship. Men were prepared for confirmation and
Church Army chapels were several times used by Bishops for
this purpose. When the war had finished Captain H. J. Smith
remained in Germany for directly evangelistic work based on a
Chapel in Hamburg. He and the Reverend S. W. Betts (subsequently Chairman of the Church Army Board) were responsible for regular Christian broadcasting on the Forces Network.
Captain L. W. Chidzey and Captain A. Chambers led missions
to the B.A.O.R. in 1949 and 1965. In wartime the deepest
spiritual work was often done when a man who had seen his
companion blown to pieces, or who had heard from home
that his wife had been unfaithful, needed someone to whom
he could open his heart, and the Church Army evangelist was
there to listen. Rough statistics of the millions of beverages
served give some indication of the size of the Church Army's
work. But the motivation behind it was the Gospel of God's
love and no statistics can record how many men and women in
the midst of war found peace through the Gospel as it was
spoken and demonstrated by Church Army staff, and also of
course by the staff of the other Christian bodies serving with
the armed forces.

During the War it was not exactly 'business as usual' with
the Church Army, but much of the usual business had to go
on and sometimes under very trying conditions. The annual
conference of officers was suspended, but in 1941 four
regional conferences were arranged in London, Birmingham,
Newcastle and Salisbury. The Headquarters building in
Bryanston Street was twice severely damaged and temporary
offices were opened in the Central Men's Welfare Hostel in
the Marylebone Road.

YOUTH WORK

Not only was much of the regular work kept open, but new ventures were undertaken. In September 1940 Sister Doris Wright was appointed 'Special Children's Messenger' to the Diocese of Manchester. She was shortly joined by Sister Dorothy Knapp and the Children's Missions Department was born. Preliminary thought was given to the phasing out of the Better Britain Brigade in favour of a Church Army commitment to Scouting and Guiding which took place in 1946 under Captain A. V. Call who was awarded the Medal of Merit for his services to Scouting and Sister E. Birch. Special Crusader badges are awarded for religious knowledge. When the government developed a National Youth Service the Church Army selected a few officers for a short training in Youth Leadership and Captain John Ball opened the first Church Army Youth Centre in Harlesden in 1942. This led to the formation of a Church Army Youth Department. Plans were also made for Youth Holiday House-parties as a way of evangelism, and for the post war development of care for homeless young persons.

An Evangelistic Committee was set up under the Chairmanship of the Rev. Bryan S. W. Green, then Vicar of Brompton, to co-ordinate and encourage the work of the News Teams, the prison evangelists, the parochial officers and the staff in overseas missions. In the summer of 1942, 35 ten-day missions were held in London and Lancashire, and in 1943 a large scale campaign in Erith was concluded by a meeting at which 700 people were present. In 1944 the News Team Movement kept its tenth anniversary. A series of campaigns was conducted including a mission at All Saints' Queensbury during which 50 home meetings were on the programme. In the autumn there was a News Team Rally in the Central Hall at Westminster and a three day conference at the Friends Meeting House at which the final address was given by Archbishop Temple.

It was recognised before the war that future officers of the Church Army would need a two-year training. After the death of the Founder and the decision to build a Training College in his memory active search went on for a suitable site. In 1945 this became an urgent matter. In June of that year the

Rev. F. Noel Palmer, Vicar of St. Luke's, Prestonville, Brighton was appointed as Principal and in August it was decided to purchase a large mansion and estate on the outskirts of Reading called Maiden Erlegh. Training recommenced early in 1946 and its subsequent developments are recorded in Appendix I. Some preliminary thought was given to the provision of opportunities for retreats, refresher courses and further in-service training for commissioned officers.

TOWARDS THE CONVERSION OF ENGLAND

If the year 1942 marked the end of an era with the death of Wilson Carlile, 1943 marked the beginning of a new concern for evangelism in the Church of England. In June 1943 the Church Assembly passed the following resolution:

'That the Assembly, recognising the urgent necessity for definite action, requests the Archbishops to appoint a Commission under Standing Order XVII to survey the whole problem of modern evangelism with special reference to the spiritual needs and prevailing intellectual outlook of the non-worshipping members of the community, and to report on the organisation and methods by which such needs can most effectively be met.'

A commission of fifty was selected and sat under the chairmanship of Bishop Christopher Chavasse of Rochester. The Church Army was represented by Mr. Treacher and Captain L. W. Chidzey who for more than a year was full time secretary of the Commission. Sir Arthur Griffith-Boscawen, Treasurer of the Church Army also served on the commission, representing the Church Assembly. The Church Army provided accommodation for most of the Commission's London meetings. The report was severely criticised by those who considered that it was too much concerned with the salvation of the individual and not enough with the responsibility of the Church to society. The Commission took its lead from the Archbishop's address at its first meeting when he said:

'There is a difference of function between making men Christian and making the social order more Christian. If we have to choose between making men more Christian and the social order more Christian, we must choose the former.

But there is no such dichotomy. We must do both. Making the social order more Christian is a duty laid upon the Church, and it is to work towards the Kingdom of God. To make men Christian is also a duty laid upon the Church, and it is evangelism, and comes first in order of importance.'

The report emphasised the importance of lay witness in evangelism, and the need for training the laity, and cited the Church Army News Teams as one way of lay evangelism. It is commonly thought that the Report had little effect on the Church as a whole, but it certainly was one of the factors which contributed to the growing sense of lay responsibility which led to synodical government and to lay participation in the liturgy.

1943 was an important year for the Church Army for many reasons. Their Majesties King George VI and Queen Elizabeth visited several Church Army centres in London and honoured the Society by becoming its Patrons on 17th June. The Chairman of the Board, Mr. Frank Elgood, was knighted in the New Year Honours. There was concern about the number of Captains who had resigned for Holy Orders, thirty in number since the beginning of the war. There was controversy over a decision to transfer a number of officers from directly evangelistic work to the war work.

THE RULE OF LIFE

Another controversial matter was the proposal to revise the Officers' Rule of Life. The Church Army Rule of Life in 1943 ran as follows:

'The Church Army Rule of Life is holiness of heart following real conversion, loyal and intelligent Churchmanship, without manifesting party spirit in Religion or Politics; also realising that certain things may hinder aggressive mission-work, all C.A. Evangelists and Sisters refrain from taking part in raffles, games of chance or any form of gambling. Without condemning others, they agree to abstain from alcohol as a beverage, smoking, unwholesome reading, finery, attending theatres or taking part in dancing; also, any so-called harmless, but, to them, doubtful things.'

From the beginning Church Army officers had been pledged

to conversion, consecration and churchmanship and to absti-
nence from alcohol. Smoking had always been discouraged and
early in Church Army history its prohibition found its way
into the rule. The other items were tacked on at various times.
A committee of Board Members took immense trouble to give
all the officers the opportunity to express their views. About
65% of them replied to the invitation. As a result of the en-
quiry a more positive rule was devised and in spite of strong
criticism by a small minority it was passed by the Board in
1944 and accepted by the Society. The revised rule was as
follows:

'The Church Army Rule of Life for all officers (captains
and sisters) is holiness of life following real conversion, and
an eager desire for the salvation of the people among whom
they are set to work, for which purpose they will so conduct
their lives by the help of the Holy Spirit that they may be
better able to bring others into the fold of Jesus Christ.
Bearing in mind always the words of St. Paul, "All things
are lawful for me, but all things are not expedient; all
things are lawful for me, but all things edify not", they
will abstain from anything likely to be a hindrance to
them in their work, and in particular will abstain from the
use of alcohol as a beverage and from betting or gambling
of any kind. They will be loyal members of the Church of
England.'

The rule was revised again in 1967 by a similar process.
The current rule has only one negative clause and runs as
follows:

'Church Army Officers are members of a Church of England
Society which exists to win people for Jesus Christ by
making the love of God as revealed in him known and accepted. They accept the Society's principles of Conversion,
Consecration and Churchmembership and endeavour to
observe the following Rule of Life:

"To do the work of evangelists in the power of the Holy
Spirit, caring for people by word and action.
To order their lives after the example of Christ and to
allow nothing in their personal relationships and be-

haviour which would hinder them in making God's love real to other people.

To maintain a personal rule about spiritual discipline and devotion and the stewardship of time and money.

To undertake such study as will increase their understanding of the message of God to the people and situations to which they are sent.

To be loyal members of the Anglican Church and to work for Christian unity.

To work and pray for the effectiveness of the Church Army as a whole, and to promote sound relationships with fellow-workers." '

POST-WAR CHANGES

The years 1946—50 were years of transition for the Church Army. In this period many senior members of the Board and Headquarters staff who had been closely associated with the Founder retired or died, and new leaders came in with new ideas. In 1946 came the death of Sir Arthur Griffith-Boscawen, co-Treasurer for 26 years. He was succeeded by Lord Selborne and later by Lord Rockley. Lord Daryngton died in 1949 having been President since 1917 and actively involved in Church Army work since 1900. He was succeeded by Lord Selborne who presided until 1960. As even greater loss to the Church Army came through the death of Sir Frank Elgood in 1948, Chairman of both Church Army and Church Army Housing and Controller of Church Army properties, and a co-Treasurer. His mantle fell on four separate people. Major-General Sir Colin Jardine took the Church Army Chair and Mr. A. T. Pike the Housing Chair. Mr. A. F. Bone became Treasurer and Mr. Anders Mathiesen Controller of Properties. Miss J. S. Walker left the Board in 1950 after 34 years as an active member. In 1946 Miss Leech passed the leadership of the Women's Work to Miss Katherine Inglis. Heads of Departments who retired included Deaconess Benniston, Deaconess Ruddle, and Captains Gardham and Hazle. Mr. J. S. F. Parker succeeded Mr. Cutlack as Chief Accountant. In June 1949 the Rev. H. B. Brewer who had been a Captain and a Board member and had become Principal of the Training College when the Rev. Noel Palmer resigned, was followed as Principal

by the Rev. Neil L. Pritchard. In September 1949 Prebendary
Treacher, who had borne the brunt of many of the changes,
and had steered the Church Army through one of its critical
periods, felt bound to resign because of his repeated and
serious illness. He retained one link with the Church Army for
several years, viz. in the counselling of professional men who
had got themselves into trouble and had to give up their
profession, clergy, doctors, lawyers, teachers. This was a work
which Captain Walter Spencer had pioneered and which was
subsequently continued at a suburban house called Spencer
Lodge where some of the men lived.

On 9th December, 1951 came the death of Marie Louise
Carlile, Sister of the Founder, at the age of 90. She had been
retired for some years, but most of the Church Army Sisters
regarded her as their leader and friend. As her memorial
states, 'She helped her brother to create the Church Army and
opened a door for the training of women for whole-time
service in the Church. Through her selfless life and devotion
to her Lord countless lives were enriched and brought from
darkness to Light.'

A few links with the War years are worth recording. In the
1946 New Year Honours list the names of nine Church Army
officers and non-commissioned workers appeared. In March
Sister M. E. J. Pegg was highly commended by the G.O.C. in
Egypt. A dispute had arisen between some British soldiers
waiting for a bus at Fort Tewfik and an Egyptian guard who
were prepared to use bayonets. The communique said 'For
forty minutes she kept four infuriated Egyptians at bay in the
guard room at the C.A. Institute. This was in keeping with the
highest tradition of British womanhood, and prevented a
serious incident and possible loss of life.' Captain and Mrs.
Gardner revived a service which the Church Army had given
after the first World War viz. organised visits of relatives to
the graves of men who had fallen. Captain and Mrs. Gardner
had the necessary knowledge of continental travel and the
sensitivity which such delicate work required. They also made
the hospitality arrangements on both sides of the Channel and
escorted 70 groups personally to 26 cemeteries.

Fresh links were formed with the autonomous societies
overseas. Captain Ding was commissioned as Director of the

Church Army in Canada, but there was little to direct because in 1949 there were only five active officers. His successor Captain Raymond Taylor, with immense energy and persistence, was able to build on Captain Ding's work and establish a strong body of evangelists. Captain F. C. Pearce's appointment as Director of the New Zealand Church Army was approved by the English Board. He was one of four English officers and 25 New Zealand officers serving in 1949. Captain A. Batley went to Australia in 1950 and became Federal Secretary in the following year. A number of new missionaries were sent to supplement and in some cases replace Church Army staff in South Africa, Tanganyika, India and until 1951 in China.

An important development of Church Army work took place after the war in the field of old people's welfare. Church Army hostels had always included the elderly among their residents. Between the wars a few Anchorage Homes for men at Fleet, Tunbridge Wells and Brighton, and Sunset Homes for women at Bootle, Bovey Tracy and Bournemouth, had been opened to provide for elderly people who could no longer live independently. Several more Sunset Homes, at Woking, Lowestoft and Putney, and an Anchorage Home at Newport, Isle of Wight, were added before 1950. But there were many elderly people who were capable of living on their own and looking after themselves if suitable accommodation was available. Many a family had an elderly parent living with them during the war. There was enough room while the husband was away in the Army and the children were small. But after the war there was no longer room for Granny. And so in 1945 Church Army and Church Army Housing decided to acquire large houses and convert each of them into approximately a dozen flatlets. Each resident was to have a bed-sitting room with a kitchen unit, and toilet accommodation would be shared. A warden would keep a very unobtrusive eye on the residents.

Sir Winston Churchill gave his name to the scheme and his daughter Mary (now Lady Soames) took a very active part in the scheme and personally opened more than fifty of the houses. The scheme was launched at a meeting in Grosvenor House in February 1946, and by the end of the year 25 houses scattered throughout England were in the process of conversion.

In the post war years the Church Army expanded its Visual Aid Department. Prebendary Carlile had made use of the magic lantern long before he founded the Church Army and for the first 70 years a large stock of religious slides was kept for sale or hire. Prebendary Carlile had experimented with cinematograph films in his services at St. Mary-at-Hill, and before the War the Church Army had made a few short films of its own work. When Captain Wilfred Thompson became secretary of the Visual Aid Department in 1950 there was already a stock of Christian films and equipment. In 1947 the Church Army purchased a Mobile Daylight Cinema Van with which Captain Dearden toured Britain, showing Christian films in dockyards, factories, promenades, back streets, playgrounds, etc. It was greatly used in London in the Greater London Commando Campaign of 1947 and Bishop Wand's Mission to London in May 1948. The novelty of this van attracted large numbers of people who would not otherwise have heard the Gospel. The van was given to the Australian Church Army in 1958. A documentary film of the Society's work was made in 1947—8 entitled *Mankind's Concern.* In the 1950's the Church Army went into filmstrips in a big way and had over a thousand filmstrips in its catalogue. Filmstrips proved more popular than moving films as a means of Christian education and evangelism.

Several of the Bishops were anxious to ensure action as a result of the Archbishops' Commission on Evangelism and its report 'Towards the Conversion of England'. In 1947 after consultation with the Church Army the Church Assembly created a Central Co-ordinating Council for Evangelism with the Bishop of Rochester as Chairman and strong Church Army representation. The Church Army agreed to be responsible for the administrative arrangements of the Council, and throughout the seven years of the Council's life contributed much practical information about evangelistic work. When the Central Council was disbanded in 1954 the Church Army set up a somewhat similar Council under the chairmanship of the Bishop of Chelmsford (Dr. Falkner Allison). While the new Council was primarily concerned with enabling the Church

Army to make the best use of its resources, it could not help relating the Society's work to the wider field of evangelism in the Church. Before it disbanded in 1957 it underlined the need for some centre where clergy could obtain information about evangelism and the resources available nationwide.

.

CHAPTER NINE

THE REV. E. W. CARLILE — 1950–1960
Younger Leadership

The Reverend E. Wilson Carlile was born in 1915, son of Mr. Victor Carlile who was the eldest son of the Founder of the Church Army. He qualified as a Chartered Accountant, and then went to King's College, London, to study theology. He was ordained in 1943 to a curacy at All Saints, Queensbury, Middlesex. This was a new housing area of some 30,000 people which had previously been an aerodrome. When Mr. Carlile arrived the district had been in existence for ten years, but it had as yet no permanent church. The team consisted of a Vicar, two curates, and two women workers, one of whom was a Church Army Sister. There were wide opportunities for evangelism, which Mr. Carlile used particularly among young people. In 1946 he moved to Church Army Headquarters as Honorary Assistant Secretary, which enabled him to retain his place on the Church Army Board which he had held since 1939. When Prebendary Treacher was ill Mr. Carlile had to take on wider responsibilities, and in the autumn of 1949 he was appointed General Secretary of the Church Army, a title subsequently amended to Chief Secretary. He was Commissioned by the Archbishop of Canterbury during the 1950 Conference of the Church Army.

Mr. Carlile believed himself to be called by God to enable the Church Army to develop its work along the lines envisaged by his grandfather. On his appointment to the leadership he said, 'While maintaining the social work of our Society, I very much want to see the expansion of our home mission work and a great increase in the number of our workers in industrial parishes. The Church Army is called to do pioneer evangelistic work, e.g. in new areas where at present there is no Church. There is still a great need for our social work, but we are also

Christian evangelists out to announce the glad tidings as well as feeding the hungry and clothing the naked. If we are going to win men for Christ, we must supply the needs of the whole man.'

Expansion there was. Requests came for officers to do pioneer work in the New Towns in England. Several new mission caravans were on the road. A new Sunset Home was opened in Hull and a Mother and Baby Hostel in Bickley for single girls who were keeping their babies, and three Youth Centres. A fine new Men's Welfare Hostel was built in Bristol as the result of the compulsory purchase of the site of an old hostel. Mr. Burdwood gave the Church Army two large properties, one at Croydon as a home for retired Sisters, and the other at Folkestone as a Church Army Conference centre fully equipped. The latter was under the direction of Sister L. Whitworth who had been a Church Army missionary in China. She managed to reach Canada during the war and ran a girls' hostel until hostilities ended. On her return to England she was the Church Army Women Candidates Secretary and then supervised the Holiday Homes of the Society which in one year accommodated over 3,000 people (including large needy families). In retirement she revisited China 50 years to the day after her first arrival there.

In 1959 Sister Brenda Macklin became the first Church Army Sister to work in the Chaplain's Department of a hospital on her appointment at the Royal Free Hospital in London.

But from the beginning Mr. Carlile was faced with the problems of combining expansion with economy. The mansion at Maiden Erlegh was expensive to maintain as well as being rather remote, and so it was sold and the Training College was transferred to a property on the corner of Cosway Street and the Marylebone Road which Princess Elizabeth had opened in 1948 as a girls' hostel. Mr. E. Phillips, the Church Army Surveyor adapted it very skilfully. The Church Army farms were no longer needed for the training of emigrants and so they were sold along with several Church Army buildings. It was decided that Tanganyika should be designated as the one overseas mission field of the Church Army and that officers serving in other places abroad where there is no local Church Army should not be replaced.

OUTREACH OVERSEAS

It was however overseas that the main Church Army development took place. Whenever Mr. Carlile went abroad he came back with some urgent request for expansion. In 1953 after visiting South Africa and Tanganyika he spent two weeks in Kenya with Dr. Leonard Beecher, the Bishop of Mombasa. It seemed to them that the Church Army with its skill in combining evangelism and social care would be an ideal society to participate in the rehabilitation scheme which the churches in Kenya were planning in the aftermath of the Mau Mau rising with all its bitterness, misery and hatred. Captain J. Ball has written, 'The major problem was the utter bewilderment of many Africans living and working (or not working) in Nairobi and who were caught up, most of them unwillingly, in the Mau Mau oath taking . . . families were broken up . . . friends and neighbours became enemies . . . After living for two to three years . . . behind barbed wire fences, with doors locked and windows shuttered there was no wonder that many normal activities of life had been disrupted.' This was the situation in which a firm request came for the Church Army to build and staff a Community Centre in one of the African housing estates in Nairobi. Four other centres were to be built in similar areas by other Christian bodies. The Bishop of Mombasa visited the Church Army Board and made a personal appeal and the Church Army agreed to send up to five officers. The first Church Army officer to begin work in Nairobi was Sister Lily Thrush who arrived in December 1954. The centre was completed by August 1956 and the Church Army team led by Captain Ball was ready for action. The development of the Centre's work and the training of Africans as Church Army officers are recorded in Appendix II.

Mr. Carlile was invited to Canada to take part in the Silver Jubilee celebrations of the Canadian Church Army in the autumn of 1954. After spending a month visiting most of the Canadian Captains he moved into the U.S.A. for ten days and met a few of the officers and members of the Board of Trustees of the Church Army. These visits did not involve the English Church Army in any fresh commitments, but his tour concluded in the Caribbean, where the Church Army had been known for many years. In Barbados he met most of the

Church Army Battalions referred to in a previous chapter and took part in open air services with up to 2,000 present of whom 90% were women. There was enthusiasm for the idea that an English officer might work in Barbados and train the Church Army leaders, but this never happened. The last connection with Barbados was in 1976 when the Rev. Winfield Collins returned to a parish in Barbados. He is a Barbadian whom the Church Army recruited as an Officer in England. He served in a parish and in a prison in England before ordination for work in his native island. The Bishop of Trinidad appeared to be very keen for Church Army work to be revived in his diocese but when Captain E. Cousins went there in 1955 he received little encouragement.

Mr. Carlile's tour finished with a four day visit to Jamaica. This proved to be the most useful of all his contacts in the West Indies, because it led directly to the establishment of the Church Army as a part of the Diocesan structure in Jamaica. In 1958 Captain Ernest Cousins was transferred from Trinidad to Jamaica. He was joined at once by Captain Roy Wilson, a Jamaican, and in the following year by Captain Noel Foderingham, a Barbadian, both of whom had been trained by the Church Army in London and together they formed a team for a Diocesan Evangelistic Mission.

SEVENTY FIVE YEARS ON

In 1953 the Reverend Neil Pritchard was appointed Deputy Chief Secretary so that Mr. Carlile could be able to devote more time to active evangelism and public relations. The Reverend D. M. Lynch succeeded Mr. Pritchard as Principal of the Training College. In 1957 the Church Army celebrated its 75th anniversary with a new colour film 'Soldiers of the Cross', two rallies in the Royal Festival Hall, a large mission in Keighley conducted by 75 Church Army staff, and the opening of a Forces Welfare Centre at R.A.F. Gaydon. Miss Elspeth M. Townsend wrote and produced a pageant of the Church Army called 'Ten Star Years and Five' (Church Army officers receive a service star for each seven years). This was followed in 1959 by her much more ambitious pageant 'Forward in Faith' performed in the Royal Albert Hall before an audience of 6,000. On that occasion the Bishop of

Liverpool (Dr. Clifford Martin) suggested that the initials C.A. meant 'Church Alive'.

In 1957 Sir Colin Jardine, Chairman of the Board, died suddenly, and was succeeded as Chairman by the Hon. Charles R. Strutt, M.A. Early in 1958 Miss Katherine Inglis, O.B.E., Vice Chairman of the Board and Secretary of the Women's Work, retired after long years of voluntary service. She was succeeded as Secretary of the Women's Work by Mrs. Jean Butlin, M.A., who brought with her invaluable experience of C.M.S. work in East Africa. About the same time the Reverend Neil Pritchard resigned to become Vicar of Holy Trinity, South Shore, Blackpool, one of the largest parishes in England. In 1958 the Rev. R. Y. Baldry was appointed Chaplain and Lecturer in the Training College and rapidly involved himself in many activities of the Church Army.

CRITICAL YEARS

The years 1958—1960 proved to be very difficult for those involved in the central administration of the Society. There was a financial crisis because of a deficiency of £73,000 on the income and expenditure account for 1957. There was anxiety about the future of Church Army Headquarters. The Bryanston Street property had only 21 years of lease to run, and a development company was interested in acquiring the site. At the same time the search was going on for a permanent site or building for the Memorial Training College. The Chief Secretary was concerned to reorganise and simplify the administrative procedure at Headquarters, and to ensure that the officers who attended Board Meetings as advisers (not having the power to vote because they were paid employees of the Church Army) would be regarded by the Board Members as equally responsible with them for the policy and management of the Society's affairs. A firm of management consultants more or less confirmed Mr. Carlile's own ideas about central administration. Each head of department had a committee which he or she was bound to consult over many details, and the committees reported to the Board. This procedure was slow and repetitive. Part of the new plan was to abolish most of the committees and give the heads of departments much more freedom of action. One new committee was set up called

Prebendary Hubert H. Treacher

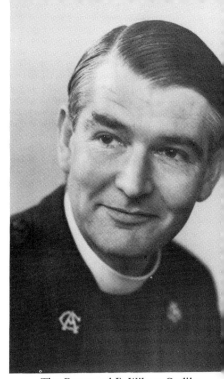

The Reverend E. Wilson Carlile,
B.D., F.C.A.

Prebendary Donald M. Lynch,
C.B.E., M.A.

The Reverend A. Michael Turnbull, M.A

London Training College, 1981

Officers commissioned by the Archbishop of Canterbury, 1981

the Management Panel which consisted of some headquarters staff (and any Board Member who cared to attend) and met weekly under the Chairmanship of the Chief Secretary. Heads of Departments reported regularly on a rota to the Panel and had access to the Panel and to the Finance Committee whenever necessary. The Panel reported monthly to the Board, and for major decisions the approval of the Board was required. This pattern which was introduced in January 1959 worked satisfactorily and gave the commissioned staff at Headquarters an increased feeling of responsibility for the whole of the Society's affairs. At a later date the field officers had the opportunity of electing two officers on Headquarters staff as their representatives on the Panel.

Matters however became complicated in the planning stage because the Board exercised its right to meet without the presence of the commissioned Board Advisers, and indeed on one occasion without Mr. Carlile, in order to discuss the new plan and to this Mr. Carlile took grave exception, because it appeared to minimise the contribution of the uniformed staff in the Society's policy making whereas he wanted to maximise it. Matters were further complicated by the Board's unwillingness to approve that the Chief Secretary should also be eligible for the Chairmanship of the Board, even though the Board of Trade had said that it would not object to Mr. Carlile being a voting member of the Board (while being a paid employee of the Society) because of his special relationship with the Founder.

In September 1959 Mr. Carlile began a tour of the Church Army work in New Zealand, Australia and East Africa. In Nairobi he commissioned the first group of eight African Captains at St. Stephen's Church, in the presence of a congregation of 600. On his return Bishop Evered Lunt who had become Chairman of the Board in June made every effort to resolve the divergence of views between the Chief Secretary and the Board, but in January 1960 Mr. Carlile resigned.

The Articles of Association of the Church Army until very recently forbade paid officials of the Society to serve as members of the Board of Management. As early as 1957 the Board had taken legal advice about changing this rule. It was not until 1972 that the Department of Trade and Industry approved that a limited number of paid servants of the Society could be members of the Board. Even then the officers could not directly elect their representatives. The Board agreed that it would elect to its membership persons chosen by a ballot amongst the officers.

Mr. Carlile's main contribution to the work of the Church Army was undoubtedly in its extension to East Africa and Jamaica and in his contact with the autonomous Church Armies in Australia, New Zealand and the North American Continent. He was given the vision of an African Society doing work amongst the underprivileged in East Africa similar to the work which his grandfather started in England amongst the poorer people. When he resigned from the Church Army he worked in two multi-racial parishes in Leicester and took the trouble to visit some of the places in the West Indies and in Asia to see for himself the original background of some of his parishioners. The first thing he did on his retirement from parish life was to visit Kenya and renew his contacts with the Church Army there with a view to raising money for the Church Army in Eastern Africa.

Mr. Carlile is a gifted evangelist in his own right. While he was Chief Secretary he exercised his gift regularly at least once a year, and sometimes more frequently by conducting a parish mission or its equivalent. He preferred to work with a team of Church Army officers, but that was not always possible, as for example when he visited South Africa in 1953. In Canada he made use of broadcasting facilities in connection with evangelism. His missions were sometimes part of a campaign in a town or rural deanery in which he led a large Church Army team operating in several parishes simultaneously. His mission addresses have a strong intellectual element as well as emotional appeal. He is often at his best as an evangelist when leading a house group in which, in the thrust of discussion, the Gospel can be explained as well as proclaimed and can be related to the particular needs of individuals.

CHAPTER TEN

PREBENDARY D. M. LYNCH — 1960–1975

Towards Democracy in the Army

When Mr. Carlile relinquished the leadership there was inevitably a period of uncertainty about the future of the Society. Many of the officers felt that the Board of Management was a rather remote body most of whose members could have personal contact with only a very few Captains and Sisters. The death of the Founder in 1942 did not have such a disturbing effect, because the war was at its height and everyone was fully stretched and also because it was known that Prebendary Carlile himself had planned to hand over to his successor. But the resignation of a leader in the prime of life was bewildering. Under the wise leadership of Bishop Lunt the Board took no sudden action. The Principal of the Training College of the Church Army has always been involved in the total management of the Society's affairs, and so the Rev. D. M. Lynch was able to combine college duties with acting as Chief Secretary for several months. The annual conference held in May 1960 helped to allay anxiety because the Board Members made themselves available to the officers, and gained their confidence. The process of selection was unhurried and it was not until September 1960 that the present writer was appointed Chief Secretary and so some of the succeeding narrative is written in the first person.

I first met the Church Army and its Founder at a students' evangelistic weekend in 1931. After my ordination wherever I worked I found myself involved with the Society. My second curacy was at St. Michael's, Stonebridge Park where I had three Church Army hostels within a stones-throw of my flat. Here I started a youth club which eventually became a C.A. Youth Centre under Captain J. Ball. My next move was to be Minister of All Saints, Queensbury, a large conventional district which had been an aerodrome. Here I had on my staff as curate the Rev. E. W. Carlile and a Church Army Sister, to say nothing of the support of a strong team of Church Army Missioners. When I moved to Tunbridge Wells in 1950 I found in my congregation a group of motherless children from the local Church Army home. Here too was a flourishing youth club to which Captain R. S. J. Sanger, the Diocesan Youth Officer, was a frequent visitor. From 1950—53 I was a part-time lecturer in the Church Army Training College and so I was not entirely surprised to be appointed its Principal in 1953.

The only innovation I brought into the College life was the acceptance of a few married men for training, who were accommodated with their families in an annexe across the road. The College had had plenty of changes since its re-opening in 1946 and needed a steady period. The College vacations provided the opportunity for me to lead several missions. In March 1955 I took the whole Training College, with some additional help from Headquarters staff, to a simultaneous mission in 17 parishes in the Medway Towns and district. In the course of seven years I got to know a great many officers besides those whom I was privileged to train. One of these was Sister Catherine Papps, a Moral Welfare Sister, based at Bromley, Kent. Her work involved frequent visits to Corke's Meadow at St. Mary Cray. Corke's Meadow was eleven acres of black mud, where several hundreds of people were living in old shacks and the backs of derelict vans and carts. I was astonished to find such a place in Kent in the 1950's. It was a place where the police never went alone, and where no post was ever delivered. Many of the people who lived there were not very keen to move because they paid very little rent and since they had no address they could remain anonymous and this suited some of them very well. Sister Papps was specially concerned about the children and young people growing up in the area. She had the courage to go in and out as she pleased and was never molested. She mustered a strong committee and lobbied the local councils, the Bishop, the M.P. and other influential people. In the end one of the councils offered to re-house the residents in obsolete prefabricated dwellings and the majority accepted the offer. New problems then presented themselves. The residents were not accustomed to paying rent regularly and many of the adults could not read: they could not see why the local council would not allow them to keep the pony for the rag-and-bone cart in the garden. And so the Church Army seconded Captain John Elliott and his wife Kathleen to live in a prefab alongside the residents and combine the duties of evangelist, social worker and teacher. All this was sparked off by one Church Army Sister. No wonder I was enthusiastic when the opportunity came to lead an Army with staff of that calibre. My main qualification for the job was probably that I already knew most of the officers personally and many of them by their Christian names.

CHRISTIAN ADVANCE

The Church Army is rather like a tree which has its main stem and branches but every year it puts out fresh shoots. 1960–61 was a prolific year. Missions were held in new housing estates, caravan sites, small villages, Cathedral cities, Broadmoor Hospital, and in several rural deaneries. The foundation was laid for a new scheme of Lay Training called Christian Advance. This was the brain-child of Captain Alan Chambers and consisted of a series of leaflets about the Christian faith and how to communicate it. Groups in parishes or deaneries met under the leadership of a Church Army officer first of all to study together one of the leaflets and then to take action as a result. The groups were not only talking shops: they were action stations. The action might be visiting the homes of Sunday School children, or calling at every house in a street with an invitation to some event in the parish or even holding an open air service. The Christian Advance scheme was developed over fifteen years and new leaflets were added to meet the needs of parish groups who wanted help over such matters as ministry to the elderly, the problems of high-rise flats, or introducing family prayers at home. As the scheme grew many of the groups met without the presence of a Church Army officer.

The various sections of the Church Army concerned specifically with young people were combined into the Church Army Youth Service which included Youth centres, Forces Welfare Centres, and Church Army Scouting and Guiding. The latter were at their peak in this period, and an annual weekend conference was held for Church Army Scouters and Guiders.

In 1961 the Church Army began to supply officers to work as stipendiary Royal Naval Lay Readers. The Church Information Office published *Express Adventure* written by Sister Margery Moore for children's missions. Captain James Johnson was the first and only man from St. Helena to be commissioned in the Society. Later he was ordained and is the only priest ever produced by St. Helena.

In the social work of the Society, Park House in Tunbridge Wells was adapted as a home for very frail old ladies, and Church Army Housing opened five new Churchill Houses. The Training College experimented with a one-year course for women between the ages of 35 and 50 to prepare them for residential work. The Society sent rapid first-aid supplies when severe flooding struck Devon. The Church Army was represented at two international conferences on Prostitution and on the Prevention of Crime. Captain F. Smith was the first Captain to serve in the Moral Welfare Department for work amongst men and boys in the Diocese of Chichester.

The leader of the Church Army inevitably finds himself in a threefold tension between the necessity for being in Headquarters to liaise with the Heads of Departments, the desire to support and encourage the field officers in their evangelistic and social work and the demands of public relations within the church and with the general public. In the Autumn of 1960 he visited all the Church Army Centres in the B.A.O.R. and commissioned the second group of East African officers in Nairobi. But he had to give most of his attention initially to two major building projects in London.

NEW PREMISES

After much negotiation with the Marylebone Borough Council permission was obtained for the erection of an eight-storey Headquarters office building on the site of the old Stingo brewery of which Prebendary Carlile had bought the freehold for conversion into a men's welfare hostel half a century before. The building was planned under the guidance of Sir Thomas Bennett (Architect), Mr. Anders Mathiesen (Church Army Controller of Properties) and a strong committee. It was erected to the specifications of the Church Army in exchange for the remainder of the lease of the property in Bryanston Street. It was occupied in June 1964 and opened by Her Majesty the Queen and dedicated by the Archbishop of York six months later.

In the autumn of 1960 the National Society announced the impending closure of St. Christopher's College at Blackheath. The Chief Secretary was familiar with the building and realised at once that it would be very suitable for adaptation and extension as the Wilson Carlile Memorial Training College. He immediately contacted the Secretary of the National Society, Canon Graham Leonard (subsequently Bishop of London), who was sympathetic with the idea that St. Christopher's would continue to be used for Christian education. The Board of the Church Army bought the property and added a modern Chapel and a block of study bedrooms and lecture rooms. The new College was opened in May 1965 by H.R.H. Princess Alexandra and dedicated by the Archbishop of Canterbury (see Appendix I).

WOMEN'S WORK

The year 1961—2 saw further changes. The Most Reverend F. D. Coggan, Archbishop of York, succeeded Lord Selborne as President of the Society, and Lieutenant-General Sir Harold Redman, K.C.B., C.B.E. succeeded Bishop Lunt as Chairman of the Board. The Reverend Canon R. W. F. Wootton, M.B.E. was appointed Principal of the Training College. A far reaching change was the appointment of Sister Janet Greene as Secretary of the Women's Work in succession to Mrs. Jean Butlin. For the first time it was recognised that a commissioned Sister should be appointed to lead her colleagues and watch over their interests and under the Chief Secretary to co-ordinate all the departments of the Women's Work. At the same time Captain A. V. Call was appointed as Assistant Secretary of the Society and personal assistant to the Chief Secretary. For many years the Sisters had outnumbered the Captains in the ranks of the Church Army, partly because no men were trained during either of the wars, and partly because the Church Army's policy of free training had attracted many women in the years before grants for further education were common. Many of the senior Sisters were at or near retiring age. Recruitment of women was becoming more difficult.

More opportunities for careers were open to women, grants for further education were available, there were by the 1950's more men in the younger age-groups, and the average age for marriage had dropped. The Church Army had always insisted that Sisters must resign from the Society on marriage. And so however strongly the importance of vocation was emphasised the fact was that fewer women were feeling a vocation to the Church Army. It was partly for this reason that in 1966 it was decided that Sisters might retain their commission after marriage if suitable work was available. Several ex-Sisters were promptly re-commissioned and today about 30% of the Sisters are married. In some sections of the Church Army men are now doing work which previously was the women's preserve (e.g. being in charge of Sunset Homes for elderly ladies). The converse is also sometimes true that Sisters are occasionally doing what only men used to do (e.g. serving as evangelists in men's prisons). In fact the rigid distinction between men's work and women's work in the Society has largely disappeared. The men and women mix freely in the Training College. Since 1963 the Archbishop of Canterbury has admitted Captains and Sisters to the same Office of Evangelist. Administratively the Society is organised according to function, men and women serving in every department.

ABROAD AND AT HOME

In the course of 1962 one of the most important decisions of the Church Army Board was to transfer the Headquarters, Training Centre and Community Centre in Nairobi to African ownership, before Kenya became an independent state. The Church Army in Eastern Africa was registered as a Society in April 1963 with Captain Ball as its first General Secretary, Mr. Max Adlam as its first Chairman and Bishop Obadiah Kariuki as its first President. In 1962 the first women candidates and the first candidates from Uganda were accepted for training in Nairobi. Although it was an autonomous body the Church Army in Eastern Africa remained financially dependent on England.

In the Spring of 1964 the Chief Secretary visited the Church Army in Canada, the U.S.A. and Jamaica and in the autumn on the same day as the Queen opened the new Headquarters he went to Nairobi to commission eleven African officers including the first two Sisters. From Nairobi he went on to Uganda to commission Captain William Bingi in the Leprosy Settlement at Kumi, which was run by the Church Missionary Society. William Bingi had been ill during his training in Nairobi but leprosy had not been diagnosed until he returned to his native Uganda. It was decided that the right course of action was to commission him to work as an Evangelist amongst his fellow patients. When he was declared clinically free of leprosy he trained as a Medical Assistant and has continued ever since as both evangelist and physiotherapist with the added advantage that the government pays his salary (even under the Amin administration!).

In October 1963 the Rev. H. J. Smith was appointed Chaplain in the Church Army with a special responsibility for helping officers in their wider study of and dealing with people mentally distressed or emotionally disturbed. Mr. Smith had been closely associated with Dr. Frank Lake and the Clinical Theology movement and brought the insights of clinical theology into the training of Church Army students and into seminars for commissioned staff and others. He trained several officers in pastoral counselling and developed a flourishing Counselling Service with two centres in London and one in Manchester. The main centre was opened by Dr. Frank Lake in 1967. In 1974 Mr. Smith became Rector of St. Margaret Lothbury and opened his second Church Army Counselling Centre in the heart of the City of London. The counselling centres deal with people who are depressed or suffering from obsessions, or who have sexual or matrimonial problems, or are victims of alcoholism or drug addiction. Church Army officers have always been involved with helping such people. For example Sister Doreen Gemmel spent 28 years of her life from 1936–64 helping women in her Bethany Room in Central London. Drinkers, gamblers, prostitutes became her friends. Many a time she met them in Holloway Prison and brought them to Bethany on their release. Captain Ronnie Rourke worked in the Spitalfields Church Crypt from 1965–74 amongst crude spirit drinkers. Captain Barry Irons from 1967–77 worked in Birmingham amongst young people who had become involved in the drug scene and in the modern revival of occultism. The tensions which arise in such work as Doreen Gemmel's and Ronnie Rourke's and Barry Irons' call for the support of the best technical knowledge and medical aid available.

A COMMISSION OF ENQUIRY

In April 1965 the Board followed up a discussion which took place at a meeting of the Headquarters staff by setting up a Commission under the chairmanship of the Right Reverend S. W. Betts, the Bishop of Maidstone, to examine the function of the Church Army in the world and the Church of today and tomorrow and the adequacy of present Church Army training to enable the Church Army to carry out its function and to make recommendations about training and further training of officers. As well as Church Army representation, the commission included the Venerable Cyril Bowles (subsequently Bishop of Derby), Miss Bridget Hill, Miss Helen Roberts, O.B.E., Prebendary Stephan Hopkinson, The Rev. Harold Frankham, and Canon Harold Wilson, and consulted with other church leaders ordained and lay, as well as maintaining a close liaison with Captains and Sisters of the Society. The Commission set up seven sub-committees to examine different areas of Church Army work. It produced interim reports in April 1966 and April 1967 and a final report in January 1968.

Immediate action was taken on some of the items in the first interim report. As previously recorded the Officers' Rule of Life was amended and permission was given for some Sisters to retain their commission after marriage. The most important recommendation of the Commission was to put into operation a new form of training which required a three-year course with a new syllabus and more modern methods of teaching, and assessment of the students by the Advisory Council for the Church's Ministry and by the Council for Women's Ministry in the Church (until these two bodies were merged). It fell to the newly appointed Principal, the Rev. Peter Ruffle, to bring the new arrangements into operation with the help of Captain J. T. Bennett, O.B.E. who had returned to England after many years of educational work in Tanzania. During the first two years after commissioning all officers were expected to take part in further training designed to develop their awareness of contemporary social problems and of new trends in evangelism and pastoral psychology. The Commission urged that experienced officers should have the opportunity of further training at appropriate levels, and of working for national qualifications where these exist. Several officers have since obtained degrees at Durham University and at the Open University.

The Commission recommended few other radical changes but it suggested that a Development Group should be formed to consider long range planning and new spheres of C.A. work. It underlined the importance of the lay training undertaken by officers in the Mission department and in the parishes and in new areas, and also of the social care exercised both by case workers and by the staffs of homes and hostels. It was particularly concerned that the Church Army should give priority in its social work to people in deepest need, and especially to youngsters in danger of addiction to drugs.

A FEW STATISTICS

The years 1966 and 1967 were typical years of Church Army work. As usual a high proportion of Captains and Sisters were based in the parishes, 150 in all, about 35% of the total active staff. About 60 were engaged in various short mission activities and lay training. 100 were in residential social work. About 30 were case-workers among families and single parents, 15 were evangelists in prisons, 15 in work amongst H.M. Forces, 15 were in charge of youth centres and 15 were serving overseas.

Most of the work was unspectacular, talking to people of the love of the Lord Jesus Christ and embodying something of his love in the care of people. The old Training College was converted into an emergency hostel for women and took in 2,500 in its first year. The men's welfare hostels received over 700 men known to have been recently discharged from prison; 1,120 men and youths on probation, 344 from mental hospitals. Extensions were built to two Sunset Homes to provide short stay accommodation for elderly people whose relatives needed to get away for a holiday. Holiday homes and the seaside camp provided rest and change for handicapped people and for women and children from families where the home was broken up or the husband was in prison or a woman had been widowed with five small children. A residential lay training centre was opened in Victoria. A Gospel Drama Group toured seaside resorts. Mission teams worked in the large summer caravan sites (one small seaside parish had 6,000 caravans and chalets and a population of 20,000 which changed every fortnight). An officer made wide use of a puppet theatre in children's evangelism. Three new youth centres were opened. The London Counselling Centre had 225 clients in its first year involving nearly 1,500 interviews of between one and two hours each. The Clothing Department helped 1,230 men with shoes and clothing, often to fit them out for a new job. Nearly 1,000 families (mothers with children) and many pensioners were assisted with essential items of clothing. 123 families were assisted with household goods and furniture to enable them to start a new home (maybe after a fire or after a prison sentence, or simply because at last they had got to the top of the Council's housing list). A colour film 'This is the Church Army' illustrated several sides of the work. Dr. Kathleen Heasman wrote the most recent account of the Church Army called *Army of the Church* with special reference to its social work. This was published in 1968. An important change of staff at Headquarters came in the summer of 1967 when Sister Lois Marsden succeeded Sister J. Greene as Secretary of Women's Work. Sister Marsden had previously worked on mission vans and in parishes and for twelve years had been Women's Warden and Vice-Principal of the Church Army Training College.

THE STATUS OF CHURCH ARMY OFFICERS

During the 1960's two processes had been going on within the Church Army. One was to integrate the work of the Church Army as closely as possible with official councils of the Church of England, and the other was to find ways of bringing the officers in the field more closely into the decision-making of the Society. In 1960 Mrs. Butlin and Captain Gardner were elected to represent St. Albans Diocese and Southwark Diocese respectively in the Church Assembly. Later Captain Michael Joint, Captain Percy Shaw, Captain Walter

Watkins, Captain Eric Heselwood and Bishop Betts, the Chairman of the Board, were members of the General Synod. The Church Army was represented on the Council for Women's Ministry, the Lay Ministries Committee of A.C.C.M. and the Committee for Social Work of the General Synod's Board of Social Responsibility and from 1968 on the Archbishops' Council on Evangelism. At Deanery level it was agreed that Parochial Officers should be ex-officio members of Deanery Synods. Several attempts were made since 1961 to secure a Canon on Evangelists, but the best that was achieved (and that not until 1975) was a clause in the Canon about Lay Workers to the effect that 'A man or woman admitted to the Office of Evangelist is thereby admitted as a lay worker in the Church'.

The most important link between the Church Army and the Councils of the Church was the participation of A.C.C.M. in the assessment of the students and the award of the Inter Diocesan Certificate to the men as well as the women, and at a later stage the replacement of the Inter Diocesan Certificate by the Diploma in Evangelism.

The problem of drawing field officers into the decision making of the Society was overdue. The Articles of the Church Army forbade any paid employee of the Society to be a voting member of the Board of Management. The only officer who ever got round the regulation was Captain Philip Prior whose salary was paid by a generous individual. For many years several Headquarters officers were appointed as Advisers to the Board and normally attended Board Meetings and were free to speak. After many attempts the Board of Trade in 1968 expressed its willingness for the Chief Secretary, the Secretary for Women's work and four other officers to be appointed as full members of the Board. Since the constitution would not permit direct election by the whole body of officers, as soon as the Articles had been amended the Board asked the Chief Secretary to recommend Headquarters officers to be elected by the Board and Captains S. W. Bickell and A. V. Call, and Sisters L. Marsden, D. King and E. Thrush were duly elected in 1972. Three years later the Board invited the officers to nominate several of their number from whom the Board would elect four to its membership. The first field officers to become Board Members were Sister Audrey Flynn,

Principal of the Josephine Butler College, and Captain David Sanderson, the Bishop of Norwich's Chaplain to East Coast holiday resorts. The Annual Conference of the Society has never had any executive powers but in 1968 and succeeding years officers have been encouraged to put forward resolutions for debate. On the first occasion five resolutions were passed on four of which action was taken. As an immediate result a Working Party was set up consisting of ten officers and two Board Members to study the organisation structure and role of the Officers of the Society. Recommendations which the Board accepted and acted upon included permission for Sisters to retire on full pension at any time between the ages of 60 and 65 if they wish to do so, and a proposal that all appointments of officers to Headquarters staff should be reviewed at the end of seven years. Most of the recommendations were about communications within the Society, e.g. the inclusion of field officers on the Conference Planning Committee, and the replacement of the 'Quarterly' News for Officers by an illustrated bi-monthly newspaper. The first edition of the new paper *Cross Swords* appeared in January 1972. The most important recommendation was that the fifteen or so Area Staff Meetings (i.e. officers working within reach of each other) should be much more widely used by Headquarters as a means of consultation with the field officers, and that an officer at Headquarters should have special responsibility for promoting and serving the Area meetings. Captain Frank Collier undertook these duties initially. Other recommendations concerned minimum standards of accommodation for Officers, the opportunities for further training, and the desirability for some officers to have sabbatical leave after twenty years service; all of which received sympathetic approval in so far as finance permitted.

MONEY MATTERS

In the early 1960's the Church Army had no serious financial problems. There was fluctuation in legacies, but taking the years 1959–1968 as a whole income slightly exceeded expenditure. There was a warning in 1967 when legacy income was low, but it was not until 1969 that regular deficiencies of over £50,000 per annum began to build up. In the summer of

1972 the members of the Board and the Management Panel decided that it would be wise policy to sell the office building in the Marylebone Road and move to the suburbs or even further afield. One suggestion was to move the Headquarters and the Training College to the budding new town of Milton Keynes. London was considered to be the best location and plans were drawn for the development of the site at Acre Lane, Brixton, where the Church Army had a hostel and industries for disabled people. Planning permission was refused at a late stage, just when inflation caught up with the Church Army in a big way and the Society was facing a deficiency of £162,000 in 1974. The Board took immediate action and in 1975 the Headquarters building was let and a move was made to a less expensive area on the North Circular Road near Stonebridge Park. A short lease was taken in an office block which faced the North Circular Road and backed on to the main railway line from Euston to the North. When the building in the Marylebone Road was subsequently sold part of the money was used for a new permanent Headquarters at Blackheath, within a mile of the Training College. It is an old property which was a school for the children of missionaries from 1857–1912 and had been used for a variety of other purposes. It is a listed building, but internally it has been very skilfully and sensitively adapted for the Church Army. It overlooks Blackheath Station which is only twenty minutes by train from Charing Cross. The new Headquarters was opened by Her Majesty Queen Elizabeth the Queen Mother on 4th December, 1980, sixteen years and one day after her daughter Queen Elizabeth II had opened 185 Marylebone Road.

Between 1968 and 1974 the Board authorised the sale of a few properties and employed professional fund-raisers with a view to substantial increases in income both for the annual budget and for capital purposes. It also took professional advice on its Press relations and publicity. The annual income rose, but did not keep pace with the rate of inflation. On the advice of the fund-raisers the Church Army formed the Concern Trust for the construction, conversion and replacement of Church Army Homes and hostels, to attract donations from sections of the community which care for people, but would not contribute directly to a church charity. The financial position improved considerably in 1975—77 but in 1978—80 there were annual deficiencies of approximately £300,000. To remedy this situation the Church Army has launched its Centenary Appeal. A substantial item in the Church Army budget is improved pensions for the two hundred retired officers who belong to the Church Army's own pension fund. Most of the active officers have been members of the Church Workers Pension Fund since 1972. A far more substantial item is the salary of the officers and non-commissioned staff who are paid directly by the Church Army. The Training College costs upwards of £130,000 per annum.

In spite of its financial difficulties the Church Army was able to initiate new projects in 1968—70. Captain Barry Irons and Captain Michael Comber founded the Birmingham and Midlands Trust for the Prevention of Addiction with the Church Army as the managing trustees and in 1968 they opened Granville House in Moseley, Birmingham, for boys at risk of addiction. They raised £20,000 for this by their own efforts. Soon afterwards the Church Army opened a similar home in Central London, at the urgent request of the Westminster Council for Social Services, to cater for a slightly older age group (16—21 years). Mr. L. F. Murphy (later Sir Leslie Murphy) raised most of the necessary funding in the City. Plans were made for a new hostel and counselling centre in Manchester. The hostel was to be for about 35 men in the younger age groups. The Board approved an annual contribution of £6,000 per annum for five years to enable a proper Training College to be set up in Nairobi for the Church Army in Eastern Africa. The capital sum could be borrowed more cheaply in Africa and annual contributions from England would cover the interest as well as the repayments. In 1970 H.R.H. Princess Margaret opened the new Elmhurst Youth Centre in Aylesbury, the cost of which the Church Army had to share.

PUBLIC RELATIONS

A number of notable events took place in 1968. Mr. Reginald Hughes completed sixty years as the Church Army's Solicitor. Sister Florence Jennett who was commissioned in 1894 was the first Sister to reach her 100th birthday (she lived on to be 104). The first Canadian Church Army Sisters were commissioned. The U.S.A. Church Army commissioned a group of Sioux Indians. 1968 was the year of the Lambeth Conference. The Church Army has always used the Lambeth year as an opportunity for contacting bishops. On this occasion every bishop who had a Church Army officer working in his Diocese was invited to a dinner and seventy were entertained. Captain John Dewdney who had been engaged in editorial and exhibition work at Headquarters was appointed Dominion Director of the Church Army in New Zealand. The Missions Department opened new work in summer holiday caravan sites in Wales and based a team of officers in East London. Captain Chambers extended the range of Christian Advance Training Aids with a course on home meetings. Captain Brian Ogden, a specialist in religious education, published the first of his three books *Eyes Right,* a children's project based on the Wilson Carlile School for Blind Boys at Buigiri in Tanganyika. Subsequently he produced *A Class of Their Own* based on the Nursery School at Nairobi. The third was a collection of modern hymns for children called *Sing to the King* which he and Miss Evelyn Wyatt compiled in 1970 including some of their own compositions.

Early in 1969 the Audio-Visual Aid Shop and the Bookshop in Headquarters were closed for reasons of economy and the space let to the Church Lads Brigade. The closure was strongly criticised because it seemed to be ending a traditional Church Army activity going back over 65 years. The sale and hire of film-strips (of which more than 1500 titles were in stock) was retained, and Mr. Andrew Risbridger, the genial bookshop manager for twenty years, became the Headquarters receptionist. Later on the Church Army set up the Westwood Studio at Blackheath for the production of tapes and cassettes. The name commemorates Len Westwood who worked for the Church Army mainly in Visual Aids for over fifty years. Captain Wilfred Thompson combined the management of the Visual Aids with their demonstration in Theological Colleges, film missions in prisons, and the organising of large Church Army rallies with military bands and distinguished speakers. Two of the most successful were in Wembley Town Hall in 1964 and the Fairfield Hall in Croydon in 1968 when the Archbishop of Canterbury presided.

In 1969 the Dean and Chapter of Westminster Abbey gave the Church Army exhibition space for six months and this brought notice of the Church Army to about 50,000 people. The Rev. Lord Sandford succeeded Bishop Lunt as Chairman of the Board but resigned in 1970 to take up a position in the Government. Bishop Betts, Dean of Rochester, followed him and retained the chairmanship for ten years. A number of Church Army officers formed links with local Radio Stations. The Church Army provided information for a Working party of the Archbishops' Council on Evangelism about 'Evangelism amongst holiday makers'.

THE WORLD WIDE CHURCH ARMY

During 1971 Prebendary and Mrs. Lynch visited all the autonomous Church Armies overseas and also the Centres in Germany. In Kenya came the final move in the Africanisation of the Church Army in Eastern Africa. A conference was held at Limuru attended by all 53 of the officers from Kenya, Uganda and Tanzania, and this was followed on 22nd January by the Commissioning of the Rev. Crispus Nzano as General Secretary by the Archbishop of Kenya and the opening of the new training college.

In Australia and New Zealand the Chief Secretary's visit was used to publicise the work of the Church Army and to encourage some of the officers working in remote areas. In Australia he shared in a Diocesan Summer School at Perth where Captain A. Polgen, an aborigine, took a leading part. He saw officers working as hospital and industrial chaplains, and met the Australian and New Zealand students in training in Sydney. In New Zealand the Chief Secretary had engagements in every diocese beginning with the Open Door Youth Club in Christchurch, which catered for drop-outs. In Dunedin he addressed seven meetings in twenty-four hours, plus radio, television, and newspaper interviews. He spent time with Captain Ingham in a Maori area, before attending a Conference of all the officers in Auckland, which included the commissioning of four officers. For part of his tour he was accompanied by the New Zealand Church Army Youth Team. From New Zealand summer he flew to Vancouver in the grip of winter.

His route took him to Prince Rupert to experience the indigenous Indian Church Army in the Queen Charlotte Islands, and thence to stay with Church Army Officers and associates in Kamloops, Calgary, Winnipeg, and Toronto. In Kamloops Captain Holmes was in charge of a men's hostel and a village church. In a home for unmarried mothers a memorable rule was observed 'Snacks : you can eat to your heart's content — you are the one who will suffer'. He and his wife had an exhilarating drive through the Rockies in a blizzard in a car borrowed from the Bishop, to fulfil engagements in Calgary. This included dinner in Calgary with Mr. Reginald Carlile, who was the only surviving son of Prebendary Carlile. The dinner took place in a club where only the men were allowed to use the front entrance. The presence of women was suffered, but they had to enter and leave by the back door!

After a few days in Toronto meeting Church Army personnel and seeing an officer at work in the Don Jail, there was a brief visit to the Church Army in New York which at that time was in the process of finding a new leader. Sister Brooke Bushong was holding the Society together pending the new appointment. The tour finished in Jamaica where Captain Cousins had arranged visits to officers all over the Diocese, including children's homes, shanty towns, an Industrial Trade Centre where an officer was training young people who had dropped out of secondary education, and Spanish Town Cathedral. On the way home Mr. and Mrs. Lynch had a few days rest with the Rev. and Mrs. Reginald Harvey in Bermuda. Mr. Harvey had been a distinguished member of the News Team staff in England before his ordination.

Later in 1971 at the urgent request of the Bishop who had known of the work of the Church Army when he was Bishop of Mandeville in Jamaica, it was agreed to form a branch of the Church Army in British Honduras. Sister Norma Thompson, a Jamaican, was seconded by the Church Army in Jamaica to lead a small team which would consist of three or four young officers from Belize who were being trained by the Church Army in London. The experiment was short lived mainly because the young officers proved unable to maintain the standards necessary for successful Church Army work when they got back to Belize.

Items of particular note in the year 1971 included the Silver Jubilee of Church Army Scouts and Guides. The Silver Acorn, one of Scouting's highest honours was awarded by Lord Maclean, the Chief Scout, to Captain Donald Woodhouse for his many years of service to boys and young men through the Scout Movement. Two Vice-Presidents of the Church Army were in the news during the year. Dean W. R. Matthews, C.H., K.C.V.O. reached his 90th birthday and Mr. W. J. MacAndrew completed fifty years as a Vice-President. The site of the Oxford Men's Welfare Hostel was sold for £105,000 and negotiations for a site to rebuild began with the Oxford City Council, which resulted after many delays in the erection by 1978 of an up-to-date Hostel for 88 men in just as central a position in the City. Meanwhile the men were lodged in a temporary hostel overlooking Christ Church Meadows. In the autumn Sir Keith Joseph as Minister for Social Services invited representatives of the Church Army to a personal consultation with him and some of his senior staff about residential care for single homeless persons.

THE NINETIETH ANNIVERSARY

1972 was the ninetieth year of the Church Army and this was marked by three major events. In May the annual conference was residential for the first time and about 350 officers and other Church Army Staff assembled at The Hayes Conference Centre, Swanwick. The Church Armies in Australia, the U.S.A. and Jamaica were represented. The President, the Archbishop of York, arrived by helicopter. Because the members of the Conference were living together some genuine communication took place between the officers themselves and between the officers and the Board members and this resulted in a new sense of mutual corporate responsibility.

In June Her Majesty Queen Elizabeth the Queen Mother honoured the Society by her gracious presence at a Reception in St. James's Palace when over six hundred guests were present including the Prime Minister (Mr. Edward Heath) the Lord Mayor and Sheriffs of London, and the Lord Mayor of Westminster. On a Saturday in September a large congregation gathered in St. Paul's Cathedral for a Thanksgiving Service which was followed by public witness to Christ in Trafalgar Square. Thanksgiving services and rallies were also held in eight provincial towns. The rallies were primarily evangelistic occasions, but they also gave opportunity for wide Church Army publicity which included the publication of four-page supplements in the *Church Times* and the *Church of England Newspaper.* Captain Percy Keirle did his share of publicity by walking from John O'Groats to Land's End in Church Army uniform with a body-banner, a feat which he repeated in 1974. During the year the Marquess of Reading succeeded Lord Rockley as one of the Society's Treasurers. Mr. W. B. D. Smith succeeded Mr. J. S. F. Parker, J.P. as Chief Accountant, and Mr. J. H. Venn succeeded Mr. E. P. Phillips as Chief Surveyor. Mr. Phillips and Mr. Smith both worked for the Church Army for more than forty years and Mr. Phillips saved the Society a great deal of money by his own draughtsmanship.

CO-ORDINATION

At the beginning of 1972 an important step was taken in the necessary process of co-ordinating and in some areas combining Church Army pieces of work which were similar in nature. Youth and Forces Welfare had already been controlled from the same office. The same Sister supervised holiday homes and Women's hostels. In January 1972 Sister A. M. Miles became responsible for all the residential homes for the elderly. Her experience of management of the Sunset Homes for nearly twenty years was now available for the men as well, and two of the homes already catered for both sexes. In 1975 a new home for 30 elderly people was opened in Brighton and named Miles Court to commemorate her outstanding work in this field. Dame Flora Robson was closely associated with this development. Sister Miles represented the Church Army for several years on the National Council of Women as well as on various councils for Old People's Welfare. On her retirement she was made a Member of the Order of the British Empire.

In 1973 the process of co-ordinating the social work of the Society was furthered by the appointment of Captain Fred Smith as the Chief Secretary's Personal Assistant for Social work. After naval service in the war Captain Smith served in parishes before training in social work in London and Birmingham and doing social work in Sussex and Norfolk. The new appointment enabled the Church Army to keep in closer touch with new thinking, new needs and new legislation in the field of social work and to maintain liaison between the Church Army and the Statutory Social Services and government departments. In October 1973 the Board agreed that three welfare departments at Headquarters should be grouped together as 'Church Army Personal Social Services', viz. Social Care (previously more generally known as Moral Welfare) Emergency Care (previously known as Women's Help) and Prisoners Families. When Headquarters moved in 1975 all the non-residential Welfare Work of the Church Army was based in Willesden where the Clothing and Furniture Department had already moved under Captain James Dearden. The logical conclusion did not come until 1978 when all the Residential Social Work was combined under one Director and all the Field work services under another, with Captain Fred Smith as General Administrator. A similar process went on in the Parochial and Missions Departments. In 1975 Captain Alan Chambers was appointed as Secretary for Evangelism. His duties were defined as Chairmanship of the new Evangelistic Committee, production of lay training material, and liaison between the various departments involved in directly evangelistic work, and between the Church Army and other evangelistic bodies. In 1975 the two selection committees for men and women amalgamated and the two uniform committees joined forces.

A notable event in the year 1973 was the opening of the new Youth Centre at East Ham by H.R.H. Princess Anne, who arrived by helicopter in a local park. The new Church Army training course had been in operation for five years and was due for a review. This took place under the guidance of Dr. Kathleen Heasman and the Bishop of Derby, and included representatives of the Church Army and A.C.C.M. All the officers who had taken the new training were consulted by a questionnaire. The verdict was favourable. Suggestions were made to simplify the Biblical material and to integrate the wives of students into parts of the course. A review of post-commissioning training and further training for officers was recommended. Later in the year the Principal resigned to become the Residentiary Canon Missioner in Blackburn Cathedral and he was replaced early in 1974 by the Rev. Richard Garrard, Chaplain and Senior Lecturer at Keswick Hall College of Education. In March Captain S. W. Bickell retired after 25 years leadership of the Men's Social Department. Mr. Robert Ewan one of the Treasurers of the Society died very suddenly and Mr. Roy Heasman stepped into the breach immediately. A few months later Mr. Anders Mathiesen, the Controller of Properties, died after 25 years of meticulous care in connection with all the buildings of the Church Army and the land on which they stood. His heart was with the people whom the buildings were to serve. He was followed by Mr. Roger Hands who had expected to be an assistant and found himself at the helm.

MINISTRY, LAY AND ORDAINED

In May 1974 the second residential Conference was held at Swanwick and the theme of the Conference was 'Ministry' and the Society tried to think out afresh its place in the total ministry of the Church and whether the Church Army would be a more effective agency of evangelism if some of its active officers were ordained. Such a discussion was inevitable at a time when the whole Church was discussing the meaning of ministry and many clergy were uncertain of their role. In preparation for the conference a special edition of *Cross Swords* was circulated and the Area staff meetings discussed the report of a group of officers in the North of England who met under the Chairmanship of Canon N. L. Pritchard, 'To consider whether in the Church of today the Church Army would be able to achieve its objects more effectively if some of its active officers were in Holy Orders and if possible to make recommendations'. They came to the conclusion that basically the status of the Church Army as a lay society of the Church should be maintained but that there might be occasions when it was desirable or necessary for a Captain to be ordained and remain within the Society. The debates at Swanwick were of a high standard and the majority of officers were in favour of keeping the lay status.

In October 1975 the Board asked an enlarged Development Group (under the Chairmanship of the Rev. Richard Garrard) 'To consider whether in the Church of today the Church

Army would be able to serve the church more effectively if some of its officers were in Holy Orders and if possible to make recommendations'. The change of wording was significant. The Committee took evidence from many officers and from ex-officers who had been ordained. The majority report can be summarised under its first recommendation viz. 'That the Church Army remains a Society of Evangelists which is predominantly non-Ordained but sufficiently flexible to have some priests among its commissioned officers'. There followed various clauses about ways and means of deciding whether an officer would function more effectively as a Priest-Evangelist. The Committee also recommended that with some provisos a Church Army Sister admitted to the Order of Deaconess may retain her commission. The Chairman submitted a minority report of one in which he dissented from the ordination of Captains. The Board acted on the majority report and a few Captains were ordained and a few Sisters made deaconesses. The matter is now under review in the light of experience.

RESOURCES, OLD AND NEW

The years 1974—5 were crucial years for the Society because of its financial problems. It seemed right to the Board to launch some new projects and to ease the financial situation by the sale of some properties which were no longer essential or suitable for welfare work. At the same time Church Army Press and Supplies (which by now consisted of only the printing works at Cowley) was sold to Alden and Mowbray Ltd., and became known as the Bocardo and Church Army Press. It was agreed that the Church Army should have a director on the Board of the new company. The Church Army retained the freehold and Mr. L. A. T. Hawes, who had worked for the Church Army for nearly fifty years was appointed Managing Director. Various steps were taken to save money or to promote efficiency. The accounting system was reviewed and in the light of recommendations a degree of automation was brought in. The Annual Conference was cancelled in 1975 and replaced by a one day meeting for officers at three centres in London, Manchester and Birmingham. Two major decisions were taken. The first was to let the Headquarters building and move to the suburbs. The other was to begin the process of letting most of the buildings which constituted Church Army Hostels to Church Army Housing. The management, work, and staffing would remain in Church Army hands. From the point of view of the public the work would still be identified with the Church Army. The advantages of the change which came about in 1976 were that full use could be made of the provision of the 1974 Housing Act relating to capital and revenue deficit grants, and that approaches to the Housing Corporation and other bodies for capital finance would come only from one body, thus avoiding the risk of confusion.

New projects included approval of the building of a new Youth Centre in Milton Keynes (to be financed mainly with public money) and the adoption in full of the National Scale for Lay Workers in the Church, with accommodation allowances where appropriate. In 1975 a new venture was begun called 'The Fellowship of the Church Army'. This was an attempt to draw into active participation in Church Army affairs non-commissioned staff, voluntary helpers, well wishers, subscribers, and supporters of all kinds. At the time of writing there are over one thousand members who are committed to regular prayer for the Society and to helping in a practical way e.g. by joining in a seaside mission or a holiday club, or visiting a Church Army home or having some fund raising activity, and to a simple rule of life based on the Officers' Rule of Life. Occasional weekend training conferences and holiday houseparties are arranged for members and their friends. The first leader of the Fellowship was Captain James Bent who was followed in 1980 by Captain Andrew Smith. A new colour film of Church Army work called 'Who Cares?' featured in particular the work of Captain Barry Irons among young people at risk of addiction to drugs and Captain Ronald Rourke, M.B.E., and Sister Theresa Capel among male and female alcoholics. In 1975 Captain Rourke completed fourteen years of service in the East End of London, four years being spent in charge of a large welfare hostel for men and ten years in charge of the Spitalfields Crypt which caters mainly for crude-spirit drinkers. The film had its premiere at the Odeon Theatre at the Marble Arch when Sir Keith Joseph and the Archbishop of York spoke in support.

LONG SERVICE

In the summer of 1974 Sister Lois Marsden retired as Secretary of the Women's Work. Her successor, Sister Elizabeth Carr, was appointed as Deputy Chief Secretary and Secretary for Women's Work. The Society had reached a stage where it was important to emphasise the wholeness of its work and to minimise the distinctions between departments, between evangelistic work and social work, between men's work and women's work. And so in addition to having special concern for the Sisters Sister Carr was made responsible for keeping under review the pension provision for all officers and the requirements of the Society for Commissioned Staff. At the end of 1974 Captain A. V. Call completed thirty years' service at Headquarters and moved to a parish in his native Devon for the remainder of his active ministry. During his thirty years he had been in charge of Scouting, the Parochial Captains and Prison Welfare, and he was a member of the Board.

The Church Army has had a remarkable record of non-commissioned staff who have served mostly at Headquarters for over forty years. In July 1974 six gentlemen attended a special luncheon. Four of them, Messrs. Eldred, E. Johnson, S. N. C. Huque and L. Westwood, were celebrating fifty years at Headquarters, Mr. Greenway topped the bill with 59 years at the Church Army Press and Mr. Frank Roberts with 57 years to his credit was still going strong and did not retire till he had done sixty five years. Officers do not usually keep their active service up for so many years, but mention must be made of Captain Vivian Budden. In October 1975 the Chief Secretary went to preach at what he thought was the 50th anniversary of St. Cuthbert's Mission Church in Coseley, near Wolverhampton. On arrival he was astonished to find that the occasion was in fact the 50th anniversary of Captain Budden's ministry at Coseley. He served in the first World War in the Pioneer Corps and was severely wounded on the Somme. The doctors said he was very lucky to survive. He went to Coseley on the day of his commissioning, 2nd October, 1925, to take charge of a Mission Church and Social Centre combined. There was much unemployment and Captain Budden kept his Centre open twelve hours a day. He ran a soup kitchen for needy families during the depression. There were splendid activities for children and young people. During the war he ran an A.R.P. post and a restaurant for factory workers and all the time he kept the Sunday Services going. He retired officially in 1960 and remained on as honorary evangelist and at the time of writing he is still active, visiting the old and the lonely, taking the service, playing the organ and preaching. 56 years in one Church Army posting is a record never likely to be broken.

In 1974 Church Army Housing celebrated its 50th anniversary. An account of Church Army Housing is to be found in Appendix III. On October 1st, 1974, a census was taken of the residents at the 21 Men's Welfare Hostels. There was 91% occupancy of the 1,455 beds available. 40% of the residents were under 40 years of age. 13% had alcohol problems, 13% were men from prison or on probation; 37% had a severe health problem (many of them having had psychiatric treatment). 18% suffered from some personality inadequacy. 60% of the residents had been in the hostels for more than a year.

ALL ONE WITHIN THE CHURCH ARMY

Early in 1975 Prebendary Lynch indicated his intention to retire from the leadership of the Church Army the following year. The post was advertised and a selection committee was chosen, and in due course the Rev. A. M. A. Turnbull was nominated to the Board, and appointed. Prebendary Lynch's final job was to arrange a Conference of the leaders of all the eight Church Armies. This took place for five days at Folkestone in the middle of an epidemic of influenza in February 1976. It was twenty years since a similar gathering had been attempted and in those twenty years three new Church Armies had come into existence, in East Africa, Jamaica and British Honduras. The discussions ranged over the whole gamut of Church Army activities including the relationship of the Church Army to the Anglican Church in each country, the place of those admitted to the Office of Evangelist in the total ministry of the church, the ordination of officers, recruitment, training, placement and welfare of officers, training of churchpeople for witness and service, the financial problems and the place of social care in evangelism. At the end of the Conference the following message was formulated for circulation to all officers and to a wider public:

'We are glad to associate Church Army throughout the world with the recent affirmation of the Archbishop of Canterbury: God Reigns, God Loves, God Cares.

We affirm the Church's continuing need for the kind of professional evangelist which the Church Army seeks to provide. We are confident that there is in the Church Army a thoroughly worthwhile career for those whose hearts have been touched by God's love for those outside the Church and that the Office of Evangelist has a distinct and recognisable role to play in the total work of the Church.

We affirm the world's need for conversion, consecration and churchmanship. We are thankful that through the ministry of Church Army evangelists individuals are brought to a personal knowledge of God by trusting in the acts of salvation in Jesus Christ and are equipped for witness.

We encourage Church Army Officers throughout the world to be equally concerned with conversion in its wider applications without which spiritual conversion degenerates into pietism. These further applications include the conversion of all kinds of need into sufficiency and the changing of any social injustices which narrow the purpose and liberty which God intends for mankind.

We have caught afresh the vision of a Society with the clear purpose of evangelism and recognise the vital place of the world-wide fellowship in the inspiration of every Officer, however isolated he may be.'

CHAPTER ELEVEN

THE REV. A. M. A. TURNBULL — 1976–1982

Latest Developments

A change in leadership marks a new stage in the life of any society. To begin with there is no immediate change in the ongoing work. A new leader begins by looking and listening and praying for sensitivity to the wind of the Spirit. The Rev. Michael Turnbull came to the Church Army at a time when changes were already in process and so he began by going back to the first principles on which the Church Army is based and stimulating throughout the Society fresh thought on the application of those principles in the life of the church and nation today.

Michael Turnbull is a Yorkshireman and he was Commissioned as Chief Secretary in Westminster Abbey by the Archbishop of Canterbury on 20th January, 1976. After curacies in Middleton, Manchester and Luton he was Domestic Chaplain to Archbishop Coggan at York from 1965—69 and Rector of Heslington and a Chaplain at the University of York from 1969—75. He was a member of the General Synod and of the Archbishops' Council on Evangelism, and serves on the Council of the Bible Reading Fellowship. Shortly after joining the Church Army he was appointed a member of the General Synod's Board for Mission and Unity.

The residential conference at Swanwick in May 1976 gave him the opportunity of meeting the great majority of the officers within a few months. A theme which recurred during that conference was that of team ministries of various kinds and of this Mr. Turnbull took note. Shortly before the Conference Mr. Roy Heasman, one of the Society's Treasurers, died suddenly. His wisdom had seen the Church Army through the financially difficult days of 1973—4. He is commemorated in the Society by Roy Heasman House, a home at Beckenham for a dozen young single mothers who are keeping their

children. After some delay during which the Marquess of
Reading held the Treasurer's fort alone, Mr. Colin Williamson
succeeded Mr. Heasman. He is a Reader and member of the
General Synod.

The main event in 1977 was the 90th anniversary of the
foundation of the Church Army Sisterhood. It was character-
istic of the Sisters that they did not hold a great meeting for
the occasion. They simply dedicated themselves afresh to their
life of prayer and their work of caring for people. There are
now more retired Sisters than active Sisters. As the Deputy
Chief Secretary wrote: 'There was a surplus of unmarried
women in the 1920's and 1930's and fewer opportunities than
there are today for full-time Christian work. This brought
many Sisters into the Church Army and this group is now
reaching retirement age.' The retired Sisters form a great
reservoir of prayer and some of them take an active part in
their local churches. An outstanding example of toughness is
Sister A. M. Sampson who recently bought herself a new
lawn-mower at the age of 98. The number of active Sisters
today is much smaller, but their variety of gifts and talents,
and the reality of devotion are just as great. 1977 was also
the 60th anniversary of the first caravan mission conducted by
Sisters of the Church Army. They took over a few vans during the first world war when men were not available. They
soon proved that they could cope with the pressures of
leadership just as well as the men. The last Sisters' caravan
was laid up in 1973.

NEW PROJECTS

Additions to the Church Army's summer programme in
recent years have been a mission on the Norfolk Broads conducted by a team who hire a cruiser for a month, and a series
of children's holiday clubs amongst the families of men serving
in the B.A.O.R. Beginning with one club in 1974, the Church
Army mounted four clubs in 1977, mainly for children aged
8—11. In 1977 about 1,000 children attended. Each club was
run by a team of 6 or 8 students and sixth formers with two
experienced leaders. The clubs lasted for three weeks Monday
to Friday, and the children were occupied all day with
swimming and gymnastics and a great variety of arts and crafts
and games. An assembly at each centre each morning gave a

spiritual content to the courses and the drama sections included Bible stories. There was spiritual fellowship within the
teams, and as much teaching and evangelism as is possible in a
children's mission. There was full co-operation by the Army
authorities, and great interest by parents not only in the clubs
but in the whole work of the Church Army.

In 1977 the Society initiated a Christian Service Scheme in
which people can undertake work for the Church Army on a
short-term commitment. Volunteers are invited to offer for a
minimum period of nine months in return for board, lodging
and pocket money. Ordinands, young people who are waiting
for further education, or are unable to find work have joined
the scheme and in the first five years about 100 have helped
the Church Army in various sections of its work and some of
them have subsequently trained as officers.

In 1977 the Church Army took over the management of the
Model Village of Bekonscot in Buckinghamshire which attracts
thousands of visitors annually. The Church Army has for
many years received from Mr. and Mrs. R. R. Callingham donations from the proceeds of the Village and now Mrs. Mary
Newman is running it on behalf of the Society. Another place
where the Church Army undertook new responsibility was the
Youth Adventure Centre at Sheldon in Devon on the edge of
Dartmoor. The Church Army took it over from a trust and
has developed its work under the leadership of Captain and
Mrs. Carl Lee. The centre is used by many school parties who
are interested in the study of natural life and geology, and
provides many opportunities of evangelism among the 4000
who use Sheldon each year. In 1978 an Open Air Theatre was
prepared and 'Comfort ye my people' was performed before
1700 people in all.

TEAM WORK

1977 might well be described as a 'Year of the Team' for
the Church Army. There were five mobile mission teams in
operation, one in the North of England and one in the South,
one in Wales, one in Taunton and one based in Northern
Ireland, but often to be found south of the border. Throughout the troubles in Ulster a group of Church Army officers,
under the leadership of Captain Deane Stewart of Enniskillen
have maintained a steady evangelistic work. The most senior

members of the team are Captain and Sister Gregg. Captain
Gregg led the Church Army in New Zealand 1956–1963. Early
in 1978 a large team including the Chief Secretary led a
series of missions in the Armagh Diocese. Towards the end of
1977 Urban Teams were set up, with a group of officers
working in a town or part of a town, combining evangelistic
and social work skills. Many of the places selected were inner
city areas or places where church life was at a very low ebb,
in Hull, Darlington, Manchester, the Black Country. More
recently two young Captains have begun work in a difficult
area of Woolwich. The teams all live with the vandalism, and
race prejudice and fear which most of us see only on the
television screen. Sister Audrey Shilling has worked for several
years in the East End of London partly at Oxford House and
more recently as a member of the Stepney Action Research
Team (START). Her experience of trying to communicate the
Gospel as good news and to build up Christian groups in a
working class culture has been embodied in a booklet *Church
Army and Urban Missions.*

Captain Dennis Oxley leader of the Northern Mission Team
described in vivid terms the variety and encouragement of
Mission work:

' "Variety is the spice of life", or so it is said. Certainly
the Northern Mission Team never lacked variety. One week
in an inner-city parish with a vast church beautifully sand-
blasted, and another week a rural parish with three tiny
gems of churches. One week with High Mass and Benedic-
tion and another with Morning and Evening Prayer and
North End at the Lord's Supper. In one parish a Teaching
Week, in another an Evangelistic Mission. Sometimes working as a Team on our own, sometimes with other colleagues
from the Mission Department or with a priest from a
monastic order and a Baptist minister. Sometimes a united
Mission with Churches of other denominations, sometimes
with the Anglican Church alone.

But wherever we go our main concern is with people;
God created people. God became Man in the Person of
Jesus Christ, and he died for people. God the Holy Spirit
can make God's power and the grace of the Lord Jesus
effective in the lives of people. So people matter to us, because they matter to God, as we matter to God.

Those people may be a family of four living in one room in a large house divided into twenty one-roomed flats with shared toilets, or they may be two-car families in a very different parish, but they matter to God.

No longer can the Church regard a parish Mission as a time when they call in the experts to do the job for them but as a time when they invite the Missioners to come and help them in the work of Mission in the Parish. If there is one word that describes the work of the Northern Mission Team better than any other, it is "Encouragement".

The Church, the people of God, are encouraged through a Parish Mission. At a home meeting people are encouraged as they hear one another speak of their faith in God and in Christ. Many a person has been surprised by hearing himself speak of his Christian convictions in a small group.

Elderly people, housebound, are often greatly encouraged when one of the Team visits them, listens, chats and prays with them.

The enthusiasm of the young ones attending the Children's Specials is often like electricity pulsating through the lines of contact in the Parish. The sight of mothers and fathers too, sitting in with younger children at their meetings, is frequently a cause of encouragement.

Encouragement comes when God the Holy Spirit is at work, assuring people of God, making Jesus real in life today.'

While all this was going on the Chief Secretary was considering what changes of structure in the Society would help to provide better support for officers, and enable better communication within the Society. He wanted to release Departmental Heads from administrative chores and set them free to exercise pastoral care of their officers, and to pass on information about resources that are available. He saw the Area Staff meetings (which only about 50% of officers attended regularly) as being a vital link between Headquarters on the one hand and the field officers and their constituencies on the other hand. The four existing main committees of the Church Army (under the Board) viz. Finance and Property, Evangelistic, Social and Training, needed to be supplemented by a Communications Committee responsible for exhibitions, public relations of all kinds, filmstrips etc., and a Personnel

Committee with special concern for Area Staff Meetings, the Church Army Fellowship, the Church Army Conference and the care of retired officers. In the following year these committees were formed, four of them under the Chairmanship of Assistant Chief Secretaries, Captain Chambers (Evangelism), Captain F. Smith (Social Work), Deaconess M. Parsons (Personnel) and Captain D. Woodhouse (Communications). The Treasurer chaired the Finance Committee and Mr. B. Worrall chaired the Training Committee.

PUBLIC RELATIONS

1978 was a year notable for many events in the life of the Church Army and for the personalities connected with them. On March 3rd H.R.H. Princess Alice, Duchess of Gloucester, opened the Mathiesen Youth and Community Centre in Milton Keynes. She described it as a place where young people could meet their friends and where they could face up to the challenge of serving the Lord Jesus Christ. Within a few months there was a regular membership of 350 young people with such activities as hair styling, football, skateboarding, cookery, keep fit, motor cycle maintenance, canoemaking, arts and crafts as well as the usual indoor games. The centre is open most of the day and seven days a week and it caters for all ages from a pre-school playgroup to the Evergreen Club. Captain R. Bussell, the first Warden, says 'We always close the Centre with an epilogue, and it is nearly always well attended'.

In June a great Flower Festival in aid of the Church Army was held at Hovingham Hall and Church in Yorkshire. It is reckoned that 10,000 people not only enjoyed the flowers, but also learned a great deal about the Church Army and the Society's funds benefited to the extent of £5,000. The Festival included the Premiere of a new venture into Evangelism, a multi-media musical called 'Which Way?'. It is intended to be performed before non-Christian audiences in non-religious venues.

Later in June, Roy Heasman House was officially opened by Dr. Kathleen Heasman. In October Sir Leslie Murphy (who was knighted during the year) opened Lucy Faithfull House, the new Men's Welfare Hostel in Oxford, a city in which the

Church Army has been active since 1883. Baroness Lucy Faithfull chaired the committee which had raised £40,000 for amenities at the hostel. The facilities for the 88 men are far better than the conditions which the present writer endured in an Oxford college in the 1930's.

Church Army personnel in the news included Mr. W. Wilson, the Chief Cashier, and Mr. Leslie Hawes, the Manager of the Church Army Press, each of whom celebrated fifty years of service with the Church Army, and Mr. Walter Smith the Chief Accountant who retired after 44 years with the Society. Jean Lady Jardine and Mrs. Betty Lloyd had been members of the Board for 21 years. Captain Gilbert Page was appointed as Federal Secretary by the Church Army in Australia and took up his duties at the end of the year. As well as having wide experience of evangelism and of social work he is a trained counsellor and he is the only known Church Army officer to have been a Churchwarden.

Church Army publications during the year included a booklet called 'Creating Community' which was the Church Army's response to the Archbishops' Call to the Nation and to the British Council of Churches' project 'Britain Today and Tomorrow'. 'Creating Community' was the result of consultations among members of Church Army Headquarters staff and the discussion of 'Community and Communication' which occupied most of the Society's residential conference for the year. The Chief Secretary found time to write a racy paperback *God's Front Line* about the case history of people amongst whom the Church Army works today. Recent publications include filmstrips – and in particular a series called 'Fandango', sound strips about a motor car, designed to teach the Gospel to children, and in 1980 a new film 'Front Line Evangelists'. Fresh Christian Advance Training Aids appeared throughout the 1970's. A whole series of papers have been published under the title of *Insights* on such varied matters as Rural Evangelism, Death and Bereavement, Community Living, Baptism Preparation, Evangelism and the Holidaymaker, Urban Missions, the Spiritual care of the Outcasts of society. One Church Army publication has recently been discontinued, viz. *Spearhead* which ran for over twenty years as a quarterly magazine of evangelism. It described, often in detail, many pieces of evangelism undertaken by Church

Army officers and others, and in spite of its small circulation stimulated people in the parishes to D.I.Y. efforts. It was originally devised by Captain John Dewdney and more recently Sister Winifred Rivers was the Editor.

As the Church Army moved into the 1980's and approached its centenary year a new President and a new Board Chairman took office. The new President was the new Archbishop of Canterbury Dr. Robert Runcie. Dr. F. D. Coggan had been President for almost ten years and in view of his outstanding contribution to the work of the Church Army, as a Member of the Board from 1953—56, as Bishop of Bradford and Archbishop of both provinces, he was appointed Life Vice-President. Bishop Stanley Betts, C.B.E. handed on the Chairmanship of the Board to Admiral Sir Horace Law, G.C.B., O.B.E., D.S.C. Bishop Betts had known the Church Army for many years in Cambridge, not least when he was Vicar of Holy Trinity and had the Church Army Hostel in his parish. As Bishop to the Forces he was in regular touch with the Church Army Centres in Germany. His first big assignment as a Board Member was to chair the Church Army Commission in 1965—7. During this time he became Dean of Rochester and as chairman of the Board he made himself available to all who needed his advice. Admiral Law brought to the Church Army a wide experience of administration, a concern for people, and a love for Christ which impels him to be an evangelist himself.

On June 12th, 1980 the new Headquarters at Blackheath was occupied, and proved eminently satisfactory, thanks in no small measure to Mr. Roger Hands (who moved to other work at the end of the previous year) and Mr. Peter Young, the Chief Surveyor. The new building was officially opened by Her Majesty Queen Elizabeth the Queen Mother and dedicated by Lord Coggan on December 4th. This was the second of three Royal occasions in twenty months. H.R.H. the Duke of Gloucester opened Walmer House on September 28th, 1979 as a joint project between Church Army Welfare and the Methodist West London Mission Day Centre. On April 27th, 1981 H.R.H. Princess Margaret, Countess of Snowdon, opened the new Portman House with its 21 bed-sitting rooms and other facilities for women in Central London. The work of the Society was publicly recognised in a substantial way by a grant from the Greater London Council of half-a-million pounds to be shared equally between the Church Army and the Salvation Army for the refurbishing of hostels for single homeless persons in the Greater London area.

FINANCIAL CRISIS

In 1980 the seriousness of the financial problems of the Church Army was brought home to the officers at their conference at Swanwick, and there was full discussion of priorities and of ways in which the officers could share in making decisions about the future of the Society. It was recognised that some pieces of work would have to be closed in the interest of economy and that the whole Society must be involved in the major Centenary fund-raising campaign. Men's Welfare Hostels in Birmingham and Norwich were closed. A Church Army presence in Social Work remains in Birmingham through Granville House for boys aged 14—18 from difficult home backgrounds. This is a house which is owned by the Birmingham and Midland Trust for the prevention of addiction (founded by Captains Irons and Comber). The Warden is Captain John Jordan who did similar work in Central London. One of the first places where the financial axe fell was on Church Army Scouting and Guiding, in a period when two Church Army Captains George Tearle and Ronald Bussell were awarded the high scouting honour of the Silver Acorn.

In 1981 a Centenary Appeal was launched with a target of £2¼ million for revenue and capital purposes. Some staff members experienced in fund-raising have been recruited and support has been given by several well known figures in the world of entertainment. One project was to attempt to collect 100 miles of tenpence pieces (getting on for six million coins). Another was to collect books of Green Shield stamps and many thousands of books were sent in. One bank gave £30,000. At the time of writing the appeal is making progress towards £750,000 and is being supported by parishes, schools, business houses, service units, and individuals all over the country.

FAITH FOR THE FUTURE

In the spring of 1981 the leaders of all the Church Armies (except for the Society in the U.S.A.) met in Auckland to consider their objectives and ways of achieving them. They sent the following message to Church leaders across the world:

'Church Army is there to proclaim the good news by word and action.

Church Army is there working on the edge of church life as an agent of God's change so that those whose lives are enfeebled might find wholeness.

Church Army is there to select, train and deploy lay people with the gifts of evangelism for full time ministry.

Church Army is there to build an Order of Evangelists within the Church's ministry.

Church Army is there to enable baptised and committed Christians freely to express their faith so that others may come and serve Christ in his world through the fellowship of the Church.'

As far as Britain is concerned the Chief Secretary expresses his hopes for the future of the Society in these terms:-

'The 1980's will provide the Church Army with some of the best opportunities since its foundation.

Consider our objectives:

To be speaking and living the Gospel in outreach.

To aim primarily for the poor and least privileged parts of society.

To contribute to the Church's total ministry in a mainly lay capacity.

To be most active on the fringe of institutional Church life.

Set these objectives against the background of a nation for whom the next few years will be an economic struggle; when social and human need will be ever more apparent and when the Church is responding imaginatively in flexible approaches to ministry.

It's a hard prospect but it's tailor-made for gritty and pioneering Church Army ministry.'

CHURCH ARMY TRAINING

The Church Army has always endeavoured to provide a ministry in the Church for working people who felt called to win people for Christ. Such a ministry (at least in earliest days of the Church Army) did not call for great educational attainment, but rather for intelligent people with a good ordinary education and gifts of leadership. Early recruits for training included tradesmen, miners, blacksmiths, shop assistants, clerks and factory workers. Women candidates included nurses and teachers as well as domestic servants, weavers, tailoresses and a number of young women who had never been out at work. In recent years secretaries, managers, electricians, engineers, journalists, welfare workers, local government officers, civil servants and builders have been accepted for training. Men and women have come to the Church Army from the armed services and a few graduates have found a place within the Society.

From its inception the Church Army has recognised the need for appropriate training for its officers. The first Training Home was in Oxford where the Rev. F. H. Webster gave his services as Honorary Warden. Webster had been closely associated with St. Aldates as a layman while he was an undergraduate, and was convinced of the importance of lay witness. He was ordained in December 1882 to a curacy at St. Aldates and the Rector encouraged him to give morning lectures to the Church Army Cadets. The Training Home was a converted shop which could house ten men at a time. A midday meal was provided, and for the rest the Cadets fended for themselves. The Cadets used to attend Evensong in the Cathedral before going out to their mission work in the back streets. Bishop Mackarness was the first episcopal patron of the Church Army.

In 1885 the Training Home was transferred to London and was established over a jeweller's shop at 174 Edgware Road and later at 128—130 Edgware Road, both of which were close to the slum area of Lisson Grove and to Speakers' Corner in Hyde Park. The Rev. F. H. Webster moved with the Training Home, and gave his whole time to the Church Army, editing the *Gazette* as well as supervising the Cadets until 1888. Webster formed a link with the Brunswick Chapel in Upper Berkeley Street where the Rev. E. W. Moore was the incumbent until 1887. The Church Army students had a weekly celebration of the Holy Communion at Brunswick and Webster became a regular Sunday preacher there. A subsequent incumbent, the Rev. E. G. C. Parr, was also a member of Church Army Headquarters staff. In 1893 the building became the Headquarters Church of the Church Army and functioned as an evangelistic centre under the leadership of a Senior Officer. Until the Chapel was closed in 1963 it was a regular training ground for Church Army students.

When the Church Army commenced the training of women to become Mission Nurses (subsequently known as Mission Sisters) in 1887 the students were housed in Little Queen Street, off the Edgware Road, near enough to the Men's Training Home for them to share the same lectures and combine for open-air services. The Honorary Lady Superintendent was Deaconess Turner. As the number of women trainees increased various moves were made to larger premises in the same neighbourhood. An indication of the shortage of space is given by a committee minute of 1889 that the bathroom in the Nurses Training Home is to be used during the day for prayer.

A typical day in the Men's Training Home in the year 1900 would begin at 6.30 a.m. (usually with a cold bath). Household duties preceded a chapel service at 8. Breakfast and bed making followed. There were lectures from 9.30 till 1 p.m. (with a short break). Dinner at 1 was followed by cornet or harmonium practice. (All were expected to play some instrument). A short prayer meeting was held at 2.30 and the rest of the afternoon was spent in parish visiting and *Gazette* selling. Tea was at 5 and there was time for private study till 7. The evening from 7 till 10 was occupied by public house visitation and more sale of Church Army *Gazettes*, or by open air meetings in Hyde Park and indoor services in the College Chapel (with a congregation 'fished in' by the students). Supper and prayers concluded the day. The Mission Nurses had a somewhat similar programme with some afternoon rest if they were engaged in midnight ministry to girls on the streets of Central London. Their training included several weeks experience in a hospital learning elementary nursing skills.

In 1901 both the Training Homes moved to 59–61 Bryanston Street, Marble Arch, adjoining the site acquired for the new Headquarters of the Church Army. Here the Training Homes remained side by side until they were damaged by enemy action in World War II. The Student Brothers and the Student Sisters attended the same lectures and often worshipped together, but otherwise they were kept strictly apart. Nothing was encouraged which would distract the Sisters from their vocation and if a Sister wished to marry she had to resign her commission. The first marriage of a Captain and a Sister took place in 1889. From 1889–1939 Miss Marie Carlile was Honorary Superintendent of the Women's Training Home (with assistance in later years from Miss Lacey, Miss Elsa Banfield and Deaconess Benniston). During this period several clergymen were successively in charge of the Men's Training, the Rev. Raymond Firth 1896–1907, the Rev. Edward Rainbow 1907–13, and the Rev. Dr. A. E. Richardson 1913–39 being the best known.

Initially the training given to Church Army officers was very brief, lasting only three months and in the case of the first Mission Nurses a mere ten weeks (including hospital work). The training was given free of charge to those who were accepted and in the early days of the Society money was very scarce. But as funds improved it was possible to extend the training period. Of course Wilson Carlile was accused of trying to thrust on to the parishes evangelists who were insufficiently trained, but most of the candidates had already gained experience of mission work in their home parishes and some of them were members of a Church Army Corps. The training, brief though it was, covered parts of the Bible, and the Prayer Book, the life of prayer and devotion and a great deal of practical experience in communicating the Gospel indoors and in the open air. As early as 1888 the Warden of the College was required to ascertain the individual needs of each cadet, and as far as possible to tailor the training to meet the needs. In the early days of the Social Work a few men were commissioned without residence in the Training Home. In 1910 it was agreed that in order to facilitate interchange all evangelists should have the three months training.

When the Church Army established its mission caravans after 1892 in many parts of Britain it was possible to bring about a great improvement in the training. The men came to the Training College for a short term of two weeks, and then joined a commissioned officer on a caravan for several months of mission work, with opportunity for regular guided reading. They then returned to the College for further training. Thus the whole training would last at least a year. By 1939 the process had been further extended, so that when World War II interrupted most forms of training, a two year course had been accepted as the norm for Captains and Sisters. The only exception in post war years was the introduction in 1960 of a one year course for women between the ages of 35 and 49, which equipped them for commissioning as Sisters to serve in residential work but did not qualify them for the Inter Diocesan Certificate. The short course has not been particularly popular.

Soon after the death of Prebendary Carlile the Board of the Church Army decided to launch an appeal to establish a joint Training College for men and women as a Memorial to the Founder, and also to plan for the training of its future officers when recruiting became possible. A site at Roehampton had been all but acquired when it was requisitioned for a housing estate. In August 1945 a large house at Maiden Erlegh, near Reading, with 138 acres was bought and training commenced early in 1946 under the leadership of the Rev. F. Noel Palmer with the assistance of the Rev. Donald Knight. The syllabus was geared to the requirements of the Central Council for Women's Church Work (subsequently the Council for Women's Ministry in the Church) to enable the Sisters to qualify for the Inter Diocesan Certificate and so take their place alongside other licensed Women Workers in the Church. For convenience the men took the same examinations. Because of a difference of opinion between the Principal and the Board the Rev. Noel Palmer resigned in January 1947. The opportunity was taken to draw up a detailed constitution for the Training College before the appointment of a new Principal. The Rev. H. B. Brewer who had been a Church Army Captain and a member of the Church Army Board was appointed temporarily to succeed the Rev. Noel Palmer and supervised the training for two years. On Mr. Brewer's resignation the Rev. Neil L. Pritchard became Principal. His tenure of office was marked by two important features. The first was the introduction of the London University Certificate of Proficiency in Religious Knowledge for those students who had sufficient ability. The second was the return of the College from Reading to London. Maiden Erlegh provided the advantages of quietness for study, opportunity for the male and female students to meet each other, and a variety of practical work situations. But it was a very expensive building to maintain and it was inconveniently remote from Church Army Headquarters. And so in 1952 the College moved to Cosway Street, Marylebone, to a building which had originally been a nurses home for a maternity hospital and had a large number of single rooms, and afforded separate wings for men and women. It had been considered as a possible site for a new training college in 1938. Use was also made of an annexe at 134–136 Seymour Place mainly for married students and their families. The annexe had been built as a public house and had on it the sign 'Walmer Castle' but in fact a licence had never been granted and the Church Army had acquired it and used it first as a coffee tavern and then as emergency accommodation for homeless men. It was recognised that Cosway Street was not suitable to be the permanent Memorial to Wilson Carlile, and when the Marylebone Road was widened and the flyover built to connect the Marylebone Road with the A40(M) the noise of traffic became a continuous nuisance. Many sites were inspected in London suburbs. One in Dulwich was purchased and then relinquished because of the high cost of building from scratch. In 1960 St. Christopher's College at Blackheath came on the market and was purchased by the Church Army from the National Society. The buildings already standing on the site were refurbished, a new block of study bedrooms and lecture rooms added and a modern chapel erected on the front of the site. The chapel was planned with modern conceptions of worship in mind. Its shell roof is in the shape of a hyperbolic paraboloid and is constructed of three thin skins of timber laid in different directions and is supported by its two buttresses. Long windows run from floor to roof, and are engraved with scripture texts in a modern version.

The Wilson Carlile Training College was formally opened by H.R.H. Princess Alexandra, and dedicated by the Archbishop of Canterbury (Dr. Michael Ramsey) on May 6th, 1965. The occasion was memorable not least for the personal reminiscences of the Founder given by Dr. W. R. Matthews, the Dean of St. Paul's. He illustrated Wilson Carlile's unconventionality by relating an incident in Gloucester Cathedral, 'There was a great service going on at which the Bishop of Gloucester, the austere and redoubtable Dr. Headlam was present, and also the Dean was seated in his stall. The preacher at Evensong was Wilson Carlile. At the time of the anthem Wilson Carlile erupted into the pulpit carrying his trumpet and said, "I think we won't have an anthem this afternoon; I am going to play something on my trumpet!" — which he proceeded to do. And when came the time for the sermon, that also wasn't quite in order. He said: "We've got some very eminent Christians here this afternoon. Instead of giving a sermon myself, I'm going to ask some of them to testify! Now, Bishop, you tell us . . .". Dr. Headlam, somewhat taken aback, nevertheless rose to the occasion. But I regret to say that the Dean, when Dr. Headlam had finished saying his piece, was observed to have quietly withdrawn! A man who could do all these kind of things was no commonplace person. He was a real, a wonderful human being, and a human being dedicated to Christ.'

The years at Cosway Street saw three Principals, the Rev. Neil Pritchard (who moved to Headquarters as Deputy Chief Secretary in 1953), the Rev. Donald Lynch 1953—60, and the Rev. Canon R. W. F. Wootton, M.B.E. 1961—66. Canon Wootton had been a missionary in Pakistan and in 1966 the British and Foreign Bible Society claimed him for translation work because of his fluency in Urdu and Hindi.

The next Principal was the Rev. Peter Ruffle 1966—73, who had the responsibility of bringing into operation a new scheme of training for Church Army officers, which had been devised by a group chaired by the Venerable Cyril Bowles, then Archdeacon of Swindon, and subsequently Bishop of Derby. This scheme which came into operation in 1967 extended the training period from two years to three years. The syllabus was further amended in 1976 and 1980. Two focal points in the training are assessments by the Church Army and by the Advisory Council for the Church's Ministry approximately half way through the course, and towards the end of it. Those who are passed by the Assessors are awarded the Diploma in Evangelism which has replaced the Inter-Diocesan Certificate. Each student is part of a seminar group and has a personal tutor. The teaching aims at integrating theology, devotion and service. Students who have the necessary ability are encouraged to embark on appropriate certificate, diploma or degree courses both during their college course and after commissioning. As far as possible study is related to the needs of evangelists in contemporary society so as to enable them to communicate the Gospel effectively. Methods and standards of training have of course changed over the years, but the aim has remained the same, viz. to equip men and women to serve as evangelists of the church.

The Training College has had formal supervision by the Church since its very early days. In 1890 the Bishop of Marlborough became the Visitor of the College and for many years that position was held by the Bishop of London, who until 1963 was responsible for Admitting to the Office of Evangelist. The Bishop of London always appointed an Examiner, beginning in 1890 with the Archdeacon of London for the men, and the Diocesan Inspector of Schools for the women. This arrangement lapsed when the Training College moved out of the Diocese of London into Southwark and the Archbishop of Canterbury became responsible for Admitting the Evangelists. The supervision is now exercised by the presence of representatives of the Advisory Council for the Church's Ministry at the assessment of the Church Army students as mentioned above.

In 1973 the Rev. Peter Ruffle accepted a residentiary Canonry in Blackburn and the Rev. Richard Garrard became Principal. He brought to the Training College professional skills and experience in the field of education, having been Chaplain and Lecturer at Keswick Hall College of Education.

He also strengthened the links of the College with the Diocese of Southwark where he eventually became a Residentiary Canon. In 1979 he was succeeded as Principal by the Rev. C. H. Hutchins who brought to the College a wealth of parochial experience.

It has always been the policy of the Church Army to provide its students (or cadets as they used to be called) with lecturers and teachers of proven ability. The various Principals of the Training Homes and Colleges have been supported by lecturers, whole time or part time, with theological qualifications. Some of these have been clergy who combined teaching in the College with other Church Army work. Others have been clergy and lay people who came in as visiting lecturers either weekly for a day or for an occasional whole week or fortnight. The Rev. Edward Maxlow, Vicar of Swadlingcote near Burton-on-Trent and later Rector of Great Braxted in Essex, and the Rev. F. E. Rogers, Vicar of Littleport, near Ely, functioned in this way for more than fifteen years before the first World War. Mr. Maxlow was also a member of the Executive (as the Board was previously known) for over twenty years. Mr. Rogers continued his connection with the College until 1923. Between the wars part time lecturers included Prebendaries E. R. Ford, T. Wellard and J. A. Mayo and the Revs. T. Darlington and J. C. Winslow. Prebendary Osborne was Honorary Examiner of the Sisters' College for many years. The most distinguished regular lecturer in the College in the 1950's was the Rev. (subsequently Prebendary) D. W. Cleverley Ford.

Since World War II the training has demanded two full-time tutors. The first of these was the Rev. Donald M. Knight who bore heavy responsibility for the College at Maiden Erlegh. The next to be appointed were the Rev. H. G. Holbeche, and Sister Millicent Tamplin. Shortly after the College returned to London the Rev. Ralph Y. Baldry became Chaplain and tutor and Mrs. Elizabeth Lawrence was almost a full-time member of the staff. Later the Rev. Brian E. Shephard, the Rev. Richard Parsons, and Deaconess Elizabeth Canham brought a great variety of skills to the life of the College at Blackheath.

The students in the Wilson Carlile College today have far more freedom than their predecessors of even forty years ago. The men and women mix freely together in group study and in social life. They are expected to make their own detailed personal rule of life as well as to conform to the more general Church Army Rule, and so form their own pattern of self-discipline. The mornings are still structured. There are frequent early celebrations of Holy Communion. Breakfast at 7.25 is optional. All are expected to attend Morning Prayers at 8.10 and to observe private devotions till 9, then there is half an hour of housework (still known by the traditional name of scrubology). From 9.30 till 1 there are lectures and seminars. Dinner is at 1 and tea at 6. The rest of the day is usually unstructured. Full Evensong is sung on Mondays and there is a corporate Communion on Wednesday evenings. Students are expected to spend at least 15 hours a week in private study and several hours a week in practical evangelistic or pastoral work, e.g. in a parish or hospital or youth club. Most students form a regular link with a parish in the vicinity of the College.

The basic elements of Church Army Training have not varied much. Whether the training lasted three months (as it was in the earliest days) or three years (as it is now) training has centred round chapel, study, and field work. Time is carefully set apart for private prayer and corporate worship, the latter being often conducted by the students. Study, whether in lecture room, seminar or library, has always covered a good deal of the Bible. There is a limit to what can be done in Biblical study even in three years. While paying full attention to developments in liturgy and spirituality the Church Army has endeavoured at all times to teach its officers the doctrine of the Church of England as embodied in the Book of Common Prayer. The teaching of Church History has been concentrated on the modern period. In recent years the syllabus has included a course on human relations, to help the students to an understanding of themselves and of the people amongst whom they will be working. A course on Ethics and Contemporary Society is of particular relevance in training of men and women to communicate the Gospel. The third main element in Church Army training has always been practical experience of evangelism and pastoral care, for the most part under the supervision of trained Church Army personnel. This takes up about one third of the total course.

During their training Church Army students today spend a
period in parochial work, in missions, in residential social
care and in some more specialised work such as youth leadership, prison evangelism, or service in a hospital or hospice. In
recent years attention has been given to the training of
supervisors of field-work and as a result many officers feel
that their contribution in the training of future officers has
been taken seriously. Field-work placements also result in
lasting friendships between younger and older officers and so
help to promote the family spirit and understanding which
have long been characteristics of the Church Army.

It would be difficult to exaggerate the importance of the
part played in the training by commissioned officers of the
Society and in particular by those who have served on the
college staff. Until 1939 the Resident Captain changed every
year to make sure that there was an officer on the college
staff fresh from direct evangelism, who could guide the cadets
in their practical work and lead them in Hyde Park and other
open air work. After the second World War it was felt advis-
able to have more continuity on the staff. Captain Dennis
Oxley was Training College Captain for nearly ten years and
Captain Derek White for twelve years. On the Sisters' side the
value of continuity was appreciated much sooner. Sister (later
Deaconess) Benniston and Sisters Winifred Humby, Lois
Marsden, Jean Gussin, Joan Hudspeth, and Elsie Thrush all
made outstanding contributions to the whole Society through
their work in the College.

After they have been commissioned all officers are encouraged to continue and extend their studies. In some areas
regular further training seminars are arranged. Sisters who
were engaged in Moral Welfare work in the 1920's and 30's
received an additional period of theoretical and practical
training and from 1948 onwards a number of Sisters took the
training given at the Josephine Butler Memorial House (later
known as the Josephine Butler College). In the 1960's it
became obvious that officers engaged in any form of Social
work required additional training and qualifications. Arrangements were therefore made to enable a few officers at a time
to be released from their duties to attend an appropriate course
at a College of Further Education leading to a Diploma or

Certificate either full time for a year or more, or on an in-service basis. Further study is not confined to officers in social work. Some have been able to secure places as mature students at Universities to read for a degree (usually with some theological study involved). Others have obtained degrees through the Open University. Several have qualified as youth leaders and a few as teachers. It is the policy of the Church Army to encourage its staff to develop to the full the talents and abilities with which they have been endowed not only for the benefit of the Society but also for the personal fulfilment of the men and women who have in many cases dedicated their whole lives to the service of God in the ranks of the Church Army.

AUTONOMOUS CHURCH ARMIES OVERSEAS

The foundation of the various independent Church Armies has been described in the course of this book, because they were all launched by an initiative from Britain. What follows in this appendix is some account of their development and present position.

THE UNITED STATES

The Church Army in the U.S.A. was built up by Captain Frank Mountford between 1927 and 1939 and by Captain Earl Esterbrook from 1939 to 1950, when there were about 50 officers. The number increased to a maximum of 90 in the middle 1960's The location of the Headquarters was usually in the New York area. The Training Centre moved periodically from Providence R.I., to Jersey City, to Cincinnatti, to Parishfield (near Detroit), to Brooklyn. One of the outstanding Directors of the Church Army was Captain Robert Jones who had been commissioned in 1936. He was concerned that the Church Army was becoming so closely identified with the policy of the Episcopal Church that it was doing little evangelism. Realising that the key to an evangelistic society is an evangelistic training Captain Jones transferred the training to Parishfield. This was a small community of three clergy and a deacon who were thinking independently and evangelistically and were running lay-training courses lasting from a weekend to several months. The Church Army erected its own building on the site to accommodate 18 people and made use of the Parishfield facilities and staff for a year's course for Church Army candidates. Their training was completed by a year's field work.

In 1962 the Church Army acquired the use of a large property in Brooklyn. It consisted of a Gothic church and three substantial houses together with church halls and offices. There was ample room for Headquarters, Training College, guest house, home for the Director and his family and various community activities. The Church was used for services for staffs of local firms, for services for the deaf, and for evangelistic plays and musical recitals. By this time the Church Army training course had been shortened to an intensive eight months and was directed by the Rev. William Coulter and Captain Howard Galley. The course consisted largely of group work based on non-academic Bible study researched by the students, and its aim was to help the students to understand the Christian faith in its relation to the every day problems of ordinary people. The training included pastoral and evangelistic field work in New York in churches, prisons, hospitals and homes for the elderly. After training the students went to their first posts but were not commissioned until they had proved themselves. Commissioned officers hold the National Licence of the Presiding Bishop.

The officers are all seconded to employing bodies from Alaska to Florida and wherever possible appointments are made in consultation with the National Director. But the vast size of the U.S.A. hinders personal communication and officers tend to act independently of Headquarters. The present writer once asked when he was in New York if he could see some Church Army work outside the city and he had to travel nearly 300 miles to the next nearest post. The officers do an extraordinary variety of work — teaching, nursing, vergering, residential social work in homes and hostels, especially among delinquent young people, mission work in isolated mountain areas. A few have a trailer ministry with a mobile church amongst migrant workers on building sites, etc. Many work day and night in inner city parishes with large negro and immigrant populations. Sister Flying Hawk, an Indian officer, was in charge of the youth work of Holy Trinity, Wall Street, which had six mission churches and a staff of 25 priests. Captain Hallock went to Buffalo to re-open a church which had been shut. He looked round for some obvious need in the community and discovered that backward children were not getting the help they needed in school. He went to the local College of Education and persuaded some of the students to help him give the backward children individual attention for an hour after school each day. From then on he had no difficulty in building up his church congregation, beginning with grateful parents.

The American Church Army has connections with South West Africa. Bishop Robert Mize had known the Church Army in the U.S.A. and invited a few officers to join his staff, including a man and wife who respectively taught physics and midwifery in S.W. Africa. Captain Ray Lewis, one of the first American Officers to be commissioned paid several visits to S.W. Africa to encourage local catechists in the hope that a branch of the Church Army might be started. This in fact has not yet happened. But one Namibian, James Kauluma, had a year's training in evangelism at the Church Army College in Nairobi and subsequently went to New York for further education. There he joined the Church Army and worked in several locations before going back to S.W. Africa first as Suffragan and then as Diocesan Bishop of Damaraland. He is still a Church Army Officer!

The American Church Army has always had its financial problems because it has no special constituency to which to appeal for funds, and no specific pieces of work which belong to the Church Army. All its staff are seconded. Its officers have to pay for their training. In recent years the Church Army has suffered because of a glut of clergy and it has been increasingly difficult for C.A. officers to find work. Since the Vietnam War the word 'Army' has been unpopular. And so under the leadership of the Rev. Logan Taylor in 1973 the Church Army set up the National Institute for Lay Training in the General Seminary in New York City. The Institute has trained thousands of lay people for a variety of Christian work and a few of them have been prepared there and commissioned in the Church Army under the guidance of Captain Tom Tull. The commissioned officers formed themselves into a group known as the Church Army Society with Captain Bill Paddock of Southern Ohio as its first President. For several years there was no National Director but in 1981 Captain Charles Mitzenius was appointed part-time with an office in New Jersey where he is employed in parish work.

The Board of the Church Army Society consists almost entirely of commissioned officers, with a Bishop who represents the Church Army to the House of Bishops of the General Convention. One of the first decisions of the new Board was to accept the offer of the Canadian Church Army to train U.S.A. candidates at the College in Toronto. The present strength of the Church Army in the U.S.A. is about 60 including retired officers and a few clergy who retained their commission on ordination. Captain R. W. Lewis is the current President.

CANADA

The Church Army in Canada got off to a good start in 1929 and the first group of Canadian officers was commissioned in 1930. During the 1939—45 war the number of officers dwindled and Captain Ray Taylor was faced with the task of building the Society up again from almost nothing. In 1954 there were 12 Captains and in 1964 there were 50. Because staff was small and resources few Captain Taylor got into the habit of doing everything, training the students, raising the money, doing the administration, finding the jobs, organising the publicity, encouraging the field officers, and doing the work of an evangelist himself, with the help only of a matron and a secretary. By 1964 there were two officers at the Training Centre (with a non-resident part time Principal or Warden) and two secretaries. The Headquarters office, the Training Centre, and the Director's house are all adjacent, and this makes it easier for the Director to be involved in everything that is going on. As in the U.S.A. many of the officers are either in Inner City work or in isolated places in lumber training camps. Some have to take responsibility for pastoral care as well as evangelism over large areas in parishes in the far west. Some officers do police court and prison work, some are trained counsellors, others are in charge of homes for young discharged offenders, and transients. Many of the officers have scope for evangelism amongst young people in summer camps and in Christian education. A few officers work with the Missions to Seamen. One Captain recorded 189 visits to 115 ships in a year. A regular Church Army station is at Aklavik in the North West Territory, where the officer speaks of travelling into the mountains by skidoo, stopping at every cabin. In the spring there are rat camps for trapping muskrats; in the summer fish camps, all providing opportunities for sharing the Gospel.

For many years the Canadian Church considered that their licensed women workers and the members of the Women's Auxiliary, provided the church with sufficient staff for its work amongst women and girls. It was not until 1968 that the first four Church Army Sisters were commissioned. In 1982 there are a dozen Sisters at work (some of them married to Captains).

Mention has already been made in Chapter 7 of the Church Army of Caledonia in British Columbia which is 100 per cent Indian, and according to Bishop Douglas Hambidge (now Archbishop of New Westminster) 'has the greatest impact of all the organisations and all the gatherings that take place in the villages'.

The Society kept its Golden Jubilee in September 1979 by re-enacting the original trek from Toronto to Ottawa with fifteen stops for witness on the way. The same trek cart was used and it fell to pieces on the last stage of the journey.

Captain Ray Taylor has led the Canadian Church Army for over 30 years and his strength seems to be unabated. One of his most important achievements has been the building up of groups of associates of the Church Army. These are groups of local subscribers in large towns who not only give money but meet regularly to hear and pray about the work and to support officers in their vicinity.

AUSTRALIA

The foundation of the Church Army in Australia was laid by Captain J. S. Cowland who established a Headquarters at Newcastle where it remained for 25 years. Skipper Cowland, as he was known, was in charge from 1934 to 1951 and was ordained in 1943. He was strongly supported by Sister Edith Parsons who established Church Army Women's Work in Australia. For the first ten years the Training College was also at Newcastle and moved to more commodious premises at Stockton in N.S.W. in 1941 where it remained for twenty years. Captain A. W. Batley came from England in 1951 to take over the leadership and was ordained in 1953.

He was of the opinion that the Church Army should be based in or near Sydney and so he moved the Headquarters first to Burwood in 1959 and then to the centre of Sydney in 1962. At that time there was a growing problem of parish life in the Inner City area of Sydney. Industry and commerce had taken over and many families moved to the suburbs, but many other families remained. Moreover as condemned sites were cleared new housing was built on some of the old sites and new families moved in. The old city churches had somehow to become centres of new church life. The Church Army took over one such parish, St. Michaels, Flinders Street, with St. David's, Surry Hill. The Rev. Captain Batley became Rector with a staff of three Captains and students from the Training College. This worked well for a time, but it soon became a full time job for Captain Batley and so he resigned and in 1969 he was succeeded as Federal Secretary by Captain R. L. Gwilt who had been Dominion Director of the Church Army in New Zealand for five years. Captain Gwilt is the only officer ever to have been in charge of two Church Armies. In Captain Gwilt's time as leader the Headquarters was transferred to the suburb of Belrose where it shares a site with the new Training College where Australian and New Zealand candidates are trained together. In 1978 Captain Gwilt was ordained and became a Prison Chaplain in Perth, Western Australia. He was followed as Federal Secretary by Captain Gilbert Page from London, who was commissioned to his new work by Bishop A. J. Dain in Sydney Cathedral on 9th February, 1979.

Captain Page is hoping that the Headquarters could move yet again to give the Training College additional space.

The Australian Church Army opened work amongst Aborigines shortly after its commencement, and several have become officers, including Captain Allan Polgen and the Rev. Captain Norman Polgen. Sister Muriel Stanley came from Yarrabah in 1938 to train as a Sister. She served in Children's Homes and then trained in obstetrics and became Matron of the Yarrabah Mission Hospital. She visited England for two years and qualified as a Moral Welfare Worker. She returned to Australia in 1961 for Diocesan Moral Welfare Work in North Queensland and in 1967 she was appointed by the

Queensland Government as Liaison and Guidance Officer with the Department of Aboriginal Affairs.

There are now 22 Australian Officers in active service, half of them in New South Wales. 9 are in parishes, 2 on the staff of Children's Homes, 2 in full time Youth Work, 1 in Aboriginal work, 1 in Industrial Evangelism, 1 runs a Christian Bookshop, 1 serves as a Priest-Evangelist amongst young people looking for an alternative society, and one flies a Church Army Cessna aeroplane to reach remote areas with the Gospel.

NEW ZEALAND

The beginnings of the Church Army in New Zealand are recorded on pages 71-2. Between 1935 and 1939 a number of officers were trained in Auckland and worked mainly on caravan missions in both islands. The work was largely suspended during the war and when it re-opened there were opportunities for evangelists on parish staffs as well as on the caravans. When Captain Banyard gave up the leadership in 1950 he was succeeded by another English officer Captain F. C. Pearce, who had been a member of the original team and had remained in New Zealand. The third Director was Captain John Gregg from Ireland whose term of office lasted from 1956—1963. He was responsible for the establishment of the Wilson Carlile House as a home for the elderly at Hamilton. During his leadership Captain Frank Cook and Sister Doris Wright from England spent two years with Captain and Mrs. Gregg and a team of New Zealand officers conducting missions in several dioceses. Sister Wright specialised in missions to children. Captain Dennis Oxley went from England to take charge of the training of New Zealand officers, but there were so few that it seemed wiser for the New Zealand candidates to be trained in Sydney with the Australians. After doing some mission work Captain Oxley returned to England.

Captain R. L. Gwilt was Dominion Director from 1964—68 and this was a time of expansion. He extended the Wilson Carlile House and formed the Waikato Auxiliary to support it. He introduced the Christian Advance Lay Training methods which had proved useful in England. There were new opportunities for youth work amongst rootless young people in Auckland and Christchurch. When he was invited back to Australia to lead the Church Army there the English Society was invited to suggest one of its officers for appointment as Dominion Director and in January 1969 Captain John Dewdney took office. He brought a wide experience of Church Army work in England and enormous energy. In 1973 the New Zealand Church Army Board formed the office of 'Associate Evangelist' to link with the Church Army clergy or laity who were already engaged in active evangelism. In the same year the Auckland Diocesan Synod gave parochial Church Army officers a seat in the Synod. Several Church Army officers have worked amongst the Maoris but no Maori has yet become an officer. Captain Withers had a major responsibility amongst Maoris in Nelson, Captain J. B. Ingham in Te Kaha and Sister Kathie King in Wellington. The two dozen officers between them cover a great variety of parish and mission work and there is special emphasis upon youth work, particularly amongst the under-privileged. For a time there was a travelling Youth Team, but the most lasting work amongst young people has been done in such places as the City Missions, the 'Hub' Club in Auckland, the 'Open Door' Club in Christchurch and 'Camp Helen' a youth adventure centre at Huia on Auckland Harbour. The youth work is partly evangelistic and partly social and there are several officers with wide experience in Social work. In 1981 Captain Dewdney resigned as Director and was succeeded by a New Zealand clergyman, the Venerable Brian Jenkins, Archdeacon Hauraki, who after 20 years of parochial ministry believes that the Church Army is in a unique position to serve the renewal of people and parishes throughout New Zealand.

JAMAICA

The Church Army in Jamaica began in 1958 when Captain Ernest Cousins was invited by Bishop Percival Gibson to revive the Church in Jamaica and to establish a branch of the Church Army. He was joined by Captain Roy Wilson and Captain Noel Foderingham both of whom were West Indians and had offered their services for Jamaica (see page 95). The three were involved as a team in a Diocesan Mission from

1958—60. Part of the result of the Mission was that almost every parish in Jamaica was aware of the Church Army, the Office of Evangelist was revived in the Diocese and young Jamaicans began to offer themselves for training. So far more than 30 officers have been trained in London as Church Army Evangelists and free of charge to the Church in Jamaica. The Church Army is officially recognised by Canon in the Diocese of Jamaica and has its own council responsible to the Diocesan Synod. Twelve Captains have been ordained and six of them have retained their Church Army Commission. All the officers are paid by the Diocese.

Captain Cousins is determined to keep the evangelistic element in the forefront of the work of the Church Army in Jamaica. There is a great temptation to put a Captain in charge of a parish (or 'a cure' as they call parishes in Jamaica) because of the shortage of clergy. Some of course are parochial officers, but the Church Army is primarily a pioneering society in the fields of evangelism and social care. Officers have worked in the shanty towns, Majesty Pen and Moonlight City and in the poor parts of Montego Bay which adjoin the palatial residences of the wealthy. Officers have been in charge of homes for children and young people. Captain Horace Spence opened an Industrial Trade Centre to enable young people who had dropped out of secondary education and were therefore unemployed, to learn enough about motor mechanics, or carpentry, or the hotel trade, to be able to get work. Others have been engaged in community development projects. One officer was in charge of Church youth work throughout Jamaica. A Captain and his wife (both commissioned) are on the staff of a College of Education. One Captain (now ordained) returned to England to work in a multi-racial area in South London. Some officers are mobile and available for missions, or to take charge of a church in emergency.

EASTERN AFRICA

The Missionary work of the Church Army Officers in the 1930's in Tanganyika is described on page 72. Captain Jack Bennett saw active service during the war and subsequently returned to Tanganyika to take up his educational work and eventually became Education Secretary General of the Christian Council of Tanganyika. The Church Army team in Tanganyika was strengthened by a series of Captains and Sisters and when the Rev. E. Wilson Carlile visited Tanganyika in 1953 there were fifteen officers in the field. Among them was Sister Lesley Bangham, a trained nurse and midwife. She worked in several mission hospitals and for two periods was in charge of a leprosy settlement for 350 patients and their families. Later she built her own hospital at Kalinzi in the far west of Tanganyika and ran it for fifteen years, single handed except for African girls whom she trained as auxiliary nurses. Captain Fred Varley had opened the Wilson Carlile School for Blind Boys at Buigiri, where he taught them to read Swahili in Braille, and trained them in simple crafts so that they could at least in part earn their own living. Sister Dorothy Almond turned her hand to several types of work including running a Bible school and acting as Principal of St. Philip's Theological College at Kongwa. Captain John Ball and his wife Dorothy arrived in Dodoma in 1946 and soon he found himself in charge of a large mission station at Kilimatinde with over 40 bush churches and schools to supervise.

Mr. Carlile's visit to Kenya in 1953 resulted in the commitment of the Church Army to a community centre in Nairobi (see page 94). The Church Army team comprised Captain and Mrs. J. Ball, Captain and Mrs. Leonard Straw, Sister L. Thrush and Sister D. Martin who had replaced Sister Cloudsdale who had met with a fatal accident. In 1957 Sister I. Lockett arrived to take the place of Sister Thrush who had spent 23 years in East Africa. They built up a close relationship with St. Stephen's Church which was on the main road opposite the Centre.

From the beginning there were wide opportunities of work amongst children and young people. The authorities allowed the opening of an unofficial school for 130 children of primary school age. Captain Straw and Sister Martin were experienced in Scouting and Guiding and soon active groups were registered. Classes were started in English, arithmetic, commercial subjects, and homecrafts, which helped many young people to find work. Through the children there were contacts with parents and classes in child welfare, cookery, and spinning were popular. A canteen was opened as many adults began to use the Centre. As more and more Africans poured into Nairobi in search of work shanty towns sprang up and the need for community work increased. Extensions were made to the Church Army Centre to provide a Domestic Science School and extra classrooms.

The Church Army was in Nairobi chiefly for evangelism. Regular visits were made to Nairobi prison for work amongst Africans and Europeans and to the main hospitals. Services were held in the Railway Training School which had 600 students. Experiments were made in the sale of Christian books and this developed into a large bookshop and library. From the beginning it was envisaged that Africans would be trained to form their own Church Army, but little was known of the Church Army in Kenya outside Nairobi and so a ten-day conference was arranged for selected clergy from different parts of the country, and through this the first group of candidates for training came for selection. On 11th January, 1958 eight students from six tribes including one from Tanganyika began their training. Among them were men who had suffered at the hands of the Mau Mau because of their witness for Christ. They had all had primary school education and knew a little English but the main teaching had to be in Swahili. The 'College' consisted of a flat in the Community Centre. The pattern of training was the traditional Church Army blend of worship, study and practical evangelism in the local housing estates and factories and elsewhere. The course in Nairobi lasted for a year and was followed by a year of supervised practical work in parishes after which the men were commissioned in November 1959. It was understood from the first that the Church Army would provide free training and the Dioceses from which they came would employ, house, and pay the evangelists once they were commissioned. Captain and Mrs. Dakin from Mpwapwa in Tanganyika exchanged with Captain and Mrs. Straw during 1958 and so the College had its first Principal.

In 1961 the Church Army in London decided that it was time to prepare for the Africanisation of the work in Nairobi before the coming declaration of Independence. The Church Army in Eastern Africa was registered as a Society on 2nd April, 1963, eight months before Independence, with Bishop

Obadiah Kariuki as President and Mr. Max Adlam as Chairman and Captain John Ball as General Secretary. The ownership of the Community Centre was transferred to the new Society. The English Church Army remained responsible for the expenses of the Centre and the Training College. In 1964 Captain Amos Maina was appointed Principal of the Training College and Mr. Geoffrey Macharia, Warden of the Community Centre. In 1962 the first students came to the College from Uganda and also the first women from Kenya were accepted for training as Church Army Sisters. When they were commissioned in 1964 it was seen that women have an important part to play in the total ministry of the Church.

The work of the Centre continued to grow until about 1,000 people were using it for some purpose every day. An important extension was the opening of a nursery school for children, many of whom got their only meal of the day at the Centre. Captain Ball and his team made a name for themselves in religious broadcasting.

In 1968 Sister Penina Mnjama took over the leadership of the work amongst women and girls when Sister Martin returned to England. In 1969 the Rev. Crispus Nzano who had been a Church Army Captain, and like many others had subsequently been ordained, returned to the Church Army to become Principal of the Training College. At this stage the Church Army in London agreed to finance the erection of a separate Training College on the Church Army Compound to provide facilities for sixteen students in separate rooms as well as staff accommodation and an attractive chapel. In 1971 Mr. Nzano succeeded Captain John Ball as General Secretary and in 1975 he was consecrated as Assistant Bishop of Nairobi, combining this with his Church Army work. Three years later he had to resign from the Church Army to become first Co-Adjutor Bishop and later Diocesan Bishop of Mombasa. The present leader of the Church Army in Eastern Africa is Captain Geoffrey Muiruri. The Society kept its Silver Jubilee in 1980. At that time over 60 Captains and 20 Sisters were in active service, many in parishes urban and rural, six in prison evangelism, nine as lay chaplains in the armed forces, and others in hospitals, schools, and literature work. There are only two English officers serving in Eastern Africa, Sister

Dorothy Almond at Kongwa and Captain Dennis Oxley who became Principal of the Nairobi Training College in 1981.

It is impossible to over-estimate the importance of the work initiated by Captain John Ball which has led to the commissioning of about 140 evangelists, many of whom have moved on to the ordained ministry. The Church Army is known more widely in Eastern Africa than in any of the other countries where it serves the Church.

CHURCH ARMY HOUSING

The foundation of Church Army Housing has been recorded on page 62. Until 1948 Church Army Housing was supervised by Sir Frank Elgood, an architect and an expert on housing law and other cognate matters. He was Chairman of the National Housing and Town Planning Council. The day-to-day work was in the hands of Miss D. E. Richardson (Secretary) and Mr. J. Lidiard (Estate Manager). The finance came from many sources. A few parishes gave substantial support. The Rev. J. Studdert Kennedy (commonly known as 'Woodbine Willie') interested his city congregation at St. Edmund the King, Lombard Street, to such an extent that they paid for a block of eight flats in Walworth which in recognition were called St. Edmund's House. St. Peter's Croydon paid for two houses. In Exeter Mrs. Sowton Barrow who sparked off the whole scheme formed a committee to promote Church Army Housing in Exeter. She is commemorated in Barrow Close, Winchmore Hill, where 56 family houses were erected in the 1920's with extensions later. The 1930 Housing Act hastened slum clearance: loans became available and many families were rehoused in West Ham, Mitcham, and elsewhere in London and the provinces before the 1939 war.

War brought many difficulties. Building stopped, every London estate was blasted; tenants were evacuated; vandalism occurred; the Government took up all the railings. After the war limitations on licences and shortage of materials made it necessary to concentrate on repairing damage. A few new schemes were developed including Geoffrey Close in Lambeth with 84 new dwellings of various sizes. The main thrust of Church Army Housing activity after the war was in the Churchill houses providing flatlets for the elderly (see pages

89-90). As the proportion of elderly people in the population has increased during this century it has been increasingly important to enable them to maintain their independence as long as they can and Churchill Houses provide welcome sheltered accommodation in groups of 10—20 flatlets with a warden. 77 Churchill Houses were opened by 1975, including some which were purpose built. Much of this development was supervised by Mr. Alfred Pike, O.B.E., J.P. who was twice Mayor of Finchley and was Chairman of Church Army Housing from 1948—1973. From 1973—1982 Sir Leslie Murphy was Chairman. When Miss Richardson retired in 1962 Mr. Lidiard became Secretary, followed in 1961 by Sister M. Teasdale, previously a Church Army Candidates Secretary and Moral Welfare Sister.

The appointment of Mr. A. E. H. Parsons, M.B.E., M.A., M.Sc., M.R.S.H., as secretary in 1971 led to a considerable development of Church Army Housing both in Churchill Houses and family schemes. Rapid expansion followed the passing of the 1974 Housing Act. The Ravensbourne Housing Association merged with Church Army Housing in July 1974 thus adding 195 units and sites for 232 more flats. In October 1974 the Society acquired 208 houses and 284 flats in London and the South. When the Church Army moved from its Head-quarters in Central London Church Army Housing acquired a separate Headquarters near Maida Vale, which gave space for much needed internal reorganisation. Mr. Peter Naish, A.I.H. who succeeded Mr. Parsons found himself responsible for some 2,000 family homes and 800 Churchill flatlets, with about 1,000 more units of various kinds in the pipe line. While new building still went on, the Society gave increasing attention to the modernisation of its older properties, in consultation with the residents. Regional offices were opened in Beckenham for the South East, in Waterloo for the London area, in Manchester for the North West and in Newcastle for the North East. Although the Church Army and Church Army Housing are separate bodies there is a very close link between them. Not only are two Church Army Sisters, Durrant and Watson, on the Welfare staff of Church Army Housing, but the majority of the members of the Committee of Management are associated with the Church Army. In 1977 the link became closer still because in that year the ownership of 18 Church

Army Hostels for single homeless persons was transferred to Church Army Housing, which maintains and modernises the buildings, setting the Church Army staff free for its work of welfare and evangelism. Already one new hostel has been opened in Oxford in replacement of an old building and two more replacements are in the pipeline. In 1982 Sir Leslie Murphy retired from the Chairmanship. His successor, Mr. David Cochrane, another active churchman, inherited a Society with approximately 5,000 units of accommodation, valued at £40 million with a rental income of £2 million.

BIBLIOGRAPHY

History of the Carlile Family (Paisley Branch), Private Circulation, 1909.

Edgar Rowan, *Wilson Carlile and the Church Army,* Hodder and Stoughton, 1906.

A. E. Reffold, *Wilson Carlile and the Church Army,* (an expansion of Edgar Rowan's work), The Church Army, 5th edition, 1956.

Edward Clifford, *A Blue Distance.*
Edward Clifford, *Green Pastures.* } The Church Army, 1895–1906.
Edward Clifford, *The Wounded Heel.*

R. Cholmeley, *Edward Clifford,* The Church Army, 1907.

J. C. V. Duvell, *Whizzbangs and Woodbines,* Hodder and Stoughton, 1918.

Alexander Smellie, *Evan Henry Hopkins,* Marshall Brothers Ltd, 1921.

E. Hanmore, *Out of the Depths,* The Church Army, 1939.

D. H. Barber, *The Church Army in World War II,* S.P.C.K., 1946.

E. W. Carlile, *From Canada to the Caribbean,* The Church Army, 1955.

Kathleen Heasman, *Army of the Church,* Lutterworth Press, 1968.

Graham Simpson, *A Sociological Study of the Church Army,* Oxford D. Phil. Thesis, 1979.

John Ball, *History of the Church Army in Eastern Africa,* The Church Army, 1980.

D. M. Lynch, *Action Stations,* Gem Publication Co, 1981.

The Church Times.

The Record.

Church Army *Battleaxes, Gazettes,* Reviews, Annual Reports, Quarterlies, *Spearheads, Cross Swords,* Board Minutes and Committee Minutes, *The Crusader, The Pioneer* and *Together* (publications of The Church Army in Canada, Australia and New Zealand respectively).

INDEX